TRIBUTE

ARCHITECTURE AS A FORM OF DIALOGUE
ARCHEA / MARCO CASAMONTI

EDITED BY LUCA MOLINARI

TRIBUTE

ARCHITECTURE AS A FORM OF DIALOGUE

ARCHEA / MARCO CASAMONTI

PIERO ANTINORI › ANTINORI NEL CHIANTI CLASSICO WINERY, FLORENCE
ROCCO COMMISSO › VIOLA PARK, FLORENCE
FERRUCCIO FERRAGAMO › HAND PRODUCTION BUILDING, FLORENCE
EDI RAMA, IDAJET ISMAILAJ › AIR ALBANIA STADIUM, TIRANA
ALBAN XHAFERI › ALBAN TOWER, TIRANA
SHALVA BREUS › BREUS ART CENTER, TBILISI
DANG MINH TRUONG, HOANG VU LAN › KISS BRIDGE, PHÚ QUỐC
GU JIN › ECEPDI ENERGY CENTER, SHANGHAI
DIANA LIN, STIVEN PENG › HOPE SQUARE BUILDING, TAIPEI

FORMA

EDITORIAL PROJECT
Forma Edizioni srl
Florence, Italy
redazione@formaedizioni.it
www.formaedizioni.it

EDITORIAL DIRECTOR
Laura Andreini

EDITORIAL STAFF
Maria Giulia Caliri
Monica Giannini
Beatrice Papucci

GRAPHIC DESIGN
Veronica Paoli
Deepa Mary Parapatt
Isabella Peruzzi

PROMOTION AND MARKETING
Stefano Baldassarri
Giulia Di Stefano

TRANSLATIONS
Katherine Fay

PHOTOLITHOGRAPHY
Forma Edizioni

TEXTS
Introduction and interviews
© Luca Molinari
Information, project data and appendix
© Archea / Marco Casamonti

PHOTO CREDITS
© Albi Beqiraj: p.107.
© Besart Cani: p. 145.
© Liridon Cani: pp. 116, 118-119.
© Studio Millspace: pp. 248, 257, 258, 260-261, 262-263, 264, 265, 266.
© Lorenzo Pierucci: pp. 274-275.
© Pietro Savorelli e Associati: pp. 12, 14, 19, 21, 22-23, 24, 26, 28-29, 30-31, 31, 33, 34-35, 39, 40-41, 42, 44, 49, 51, 52-53, 54-55, 56, 58-59, 60-61, 62, 63, 66-67, 69, 70-71, 72, 74, 79, 81, 82-83, 84-85, 86, 88-89, 90, 92-93, 94, 99, 100-101, 108, 110, 115, 120-121, 122, 124-125, 129, 130-131, 132-133, 134-135, 136, 138, 143, 146-147, 148, 150, 152, 153, 154-155, 158, 159, 160, 161, 163, 164-165, 190, 194, 202-203, 204-205, 210-211, 214, 215, 220, 222, 229, 230, 232-233, 238, 239, 241, 245, 246-247, 250, 267, 268-269, 273.
© Sun Group: pp. 188, 199, 201, 206, 208-209, 217, 218-219.
© Charlie Xia: pp. 220, 234-235, 236.
Edi Rama – PM Office: p.102.
Render | Archea / Marco Casamonti: pp. 166, 173, 175, 176-177, 178, 180-181, 184, 185, 186-187.

First edition: October 2024

ARCHITECTURE AS A FORM OF DIALOGUE 7

ANTINORI NEL CHIANTI CLASSICO WINERY 12
PIERO ANTINORI 14

ROCCO B. COMMISSO VIOLA PARK 42
ROCCO COMMISSO 44

HAND PRODUCTION BUILDING 72
FERRUCCIO FERRAGAMO 74

TIRANA: FUTURE PROSPECTS 102
EDI RAMA

AIR ALBANIA STADIUM 108
IDAJET ISMAILAJ 110

ALBAN TOWER 136
ALBAN XHAFERI 138

BREUS ART CENTER 166
SHALVA BREUS 168

KISS BRIDGE 188
DANG MINH TRUONG 190
HOANG VU LAN 194

ECEPDI ENERGY CENTER 220
GU JIN 222

HOPE SQUARE BUILDING 248
DIANA LIN, STIVEN PENG 250

LIST OF WORKS 278
BIOGRAPHY 284

ARCHITECTURE AS A FORM OF DIALOGUE

"[...] He who would build has to procure the architect and must generate the building with him, and then the architect will bring it into the world and, having produced it, becomes the mother of that building." We've all heard this quotation innumerable times, perhaps stated in simpler language, from the writings of Antonio Averlino, known as Filarete, in his *Treatise on Architecture*. He imagines the creation of a work of architecture as a physical act of love shared in equal measure by a father (the client) and a mother (the architect). The humanist architect views the building as a living organism, sees it grow and change in time and, as such, requiring a sentimental and carnal relationship between its parents for it to come to life.

No one before him had been so clear in delineating an equal and essential relationship between two different characters, where previously, the architect had been seen as a specialized artisan at the service of a lord and of his power, such that for many of the works built before the 15th century we have no record of the author. The Renaissance stands out, among many other things, for its recognition of the work of an author, celebrated at the time, and fought over by popes, princes and cardinals. The idea of the creative genius became so important in the 15th century as to make the artist more famous than the person who had ordered and paid for the work!

Today we are increasingly aware that every project grows out of a necessary, complex and sometimes conflicting interaction among different participants who, at various stages, contribute to the construction of a new space that will be inhabited by even more individuals, all participating in shaping the future form of the context in which it is built.

This interaction forms an ecosystem that continues to branch out and grow in complexity, and which eventually coincides with the density of the present time, but the initial spark, the beginning of it all, is always the meeting between a client and an architect. The destiny of the work and the possibility that it may play a greater or lesser role in future developments depend, to a great extent, on that initial encounter.

It is often a private occasion, with rules of engagement that change every time, in which personalities, destiny, luck, states of mind, talent and intelligence mingle, converse, enter into a natural collision to find a unique balance that will accompany and condition all the subsequent stages of ideation, project design, construction and opening to the outside world. Personally, I have always found this process fascinating, the more I have explored it, and every time I have had the opportunity to meet both the architects and their clients. Architecture has a profound inclination toward assembling materials and shaping them into buildings, which contrasts somewhat with the desire of the client to order and possess a specific work, the creative imagination and personality of the architect, the need to interact with the ambitions and skills of other experts – professionals, artisans, workers – up to the completion of the finished structure which, then, encounters the desire of its new inhabitants to live in it, change it and experience it in the difference seasons of its and their own life. Every work of architecture has the power to condense many different desires, and it is this that make the built space a living organism capable of changing with us over time, influencing our existence and our views of the world, as well as those of the adjacent community that see it, enter and inhabit it in their own, always different, ways.

For all these reasons, the idea of holding an exhibition of the work of a particular studio, Archea, in which we can see, through the words, the eyes and the emotions of some of its clients, the most important work done by the Florentine studio in the last twenty years, seems right and proper to me, because it expresses the circularity and completeness that are the hallmark of any significant work of contemporary architecture.

Traveling and interviewing clients between Europe and Asia, each different and particular, not only offers the public a diverse, wide-ranging view of the work of Archea, but above all ensures a correct understanding of the degree of complexity that every architectural studio has to deal with nowadays, when moving around the world, on scales and at latitudes that differ so greatly among them.

I traveled with the Archea team and with Pietro Savorelli, the eyes and dynamic viewpoint on these conversations, and had the opportunity to understand the richness and density of each of these works through the words of the people who pursued and profoundly desired them.

Our choice was that the majority should be constructed works, because the words had to reflect the spaces built and lived in, so as to mixed indivisibly together ideas and materials, pictures and places, dreams and reality. The words of the clients played counterpoint to the world of the Archea studio – one of the Italian studios with the most offices and branches around the world – with its work process, its key people, with the obsessions and the relationships essential to the Italian way of doing things. These are clearly identifying elements for Archea, defining the maturity of the Florentine studio, founded by Laura Andreini, Marco Casamonti and Giovanni Polazzi, in 1988, and later joined by Silvia Fabi in 2001 when it officially became Archea Associati. The interviews not only revealed fragments of the personalities of the clients and of the economic and urban history of the new buildings, but also dealt with some of the most urgent issues that contemporary architecture is going through, in a world that is changing radically all around us: the environmental and energy conversion of the works, regeneration as an urgent necessity, reflections on the significance of building new metropolitan landmarks today, and the landscape as a new horizon toward which to move with attention and awareness.

The works that represent the body of the exhibition and of this book clearly tell the story of our time and also describe the point reached by Archea's project development in the contemporary national and international cultural and figurative context.

All the works of architecture that we visited and discussed with their owners illustrate a time of change and, at the same time, can be seen as distinctive features in a context that is often fragmented and anonymous or, as in the opposite case of the Tuscan hills, the powerful statement of an original, surprising creativity.

In a historical period in which we will have to be increasingly concerned with limiting new building to safeguard the land and natural resources, every new architectural project must have a level of awareness of its role much greater than in the century just past, and this can be seen in the attention with which the client approaches a new investment and in the ability of the architect to be an active partner in this process. All the projects reviewed reflect a strong attention to the economies involved, but also to the quality of the work. The new structures exhibit awareness of their responsibility to bring quality into the daily life of the people who inhabitant them and the area around them, setting a standard they can no longer ignore.

The two projects relative to the ECEPDI headquarters in Shanghai and the Hope Square Building in Taipei, as well as the Alban Tower and the Air Albania Stadium in Tirana represent, despite the very different scale and cultural contexts, the same need to mark the territory with architecture of high formal quality and a strong environmental awareness. Each of these works reacts poetically to metropolitan contexts marked by significant urban disorder and by the lack of quality of the public and residential spaces. The responses focus on the urban character of these works, which clearly signal, with their physical appearance and size, that things are changing. The architecture of Shanghai, due to the linguistic anomaly and the character of its shapes, reflects the boxy aspect of the landscape in which it is immersed, while the Taipei building, develops around a monumental tree that becomes its symbolic heart and soul. Both are located at the intersections of major roadways with heavy traffic, generating habitable public spaces along their borders, which the local community could enjoy. The same could be said for the stadium project in Tirana, which recovers a number of important fragments of an existing building constructed in the Thirties by Gherardo Bosio – who drew up the zoning plan for the Albanian capital – radically rethinking the system of public spaces in relation to the new monument. In this case, the choice of Marco Casamonti and Archea Associati was not to produce the traditional idea of a stadium, but to encapsulate it in an urban structure that would envelope it, in which the new surface of vertical red panels and glass walls define a work of architecture capable of containing different functions and regenerating a portion of the city long abandoned. The choice to add a tower to the new stadium, neatly fitted into one of its corners, strengthens the territorial role of this collective infrastructure and clearly marks the Tirana skyline, along with the Alban Tower, the first tall building designed for Tirana by Archea, after which the studio presented its masterplan for the redevelopment of the Albanian capital currently being evaluated by Edi Rama, former mayor and now Prime Minister of the country. Both projects exhibit unusual characteristics for a typological theme widely applied on a global scale, thanks to a treatment of volumes and surfaces that functions in relation to the atmospheric dimension as a design of the external skin, interacting with the light and geometric patterns of the two buildings.

The Alban Tower was to be the first of a series of skyscrapers in the heart of downtown Tirana, and was at the same time an experimental and structural test for what is still a significantly backward construction industry context. Almost 15 years after it was first proposed, the tower now stands, overlooking Skanderbeg plaza. It was recently completed, and in the meantime many more towers have started rising around it, on the strength of its consideration as a recognizable symbol of a revolution on the metropolitan scale.

The silhouette of the Alban Tower, with its formal resemblance to the Velasca Tower in Milan and the tower of Palazzo Vecchio in Florence, is a reminder of the country's vicinity to Italian culture, and the many references that Archea has incorporated into its consolidated heritage of shapes, languages and geometries. The question of its Italian influence and of a certain fascination with the Italian Renaissance has been a constant observation with the different foreign clients, not only in the choice of the materials or in the obsessive attention to "artful construction", but also for the natural attention of the Florentine architects to the open quality of the urban spaces and of every public or private space that could involve different communities. This is a distinctive feature that has always accompanied the work of Archea, from the library at Curno to its projects in China, Tirana and around Florence, and that over the years have shaped its expression to meet different demands. A good example is the factory for Ferragamo in Florence, which restored an existing building and one that is part of a necessary action of functional, environmental and symbolic regeneration, going from the outer skin of the building all the way to its inner section. As was done in the past for the reconstruction of the market buildings at San Lorenzo in Florence, in the old harbor of Trieste or at La Valletta, where the innermost heart of the three buildings was radically redesigned without betraying the power of the existing structure. In the case of Ferragamo, the exterior treatment of the façade follows another expressive line typical of Archea, in which the metal or ceramic cladding gives the existing volume a vibrant aspect, with continuous variations on the theme of language and shape that exalt the material used and that yield harmoniously to the designers' ability to give personality to what are often anonymous factory buildings, as they did for the Perfetti factory, the Udine stadium, the Nembro library, the GEL building in Shanghai or the Liling World Ceramic Art City in China.

In many of the interviews with foreign clients, what they remarked on with rather astonishing regularity (though it really should not surprise us) was the decisive impact that a visit to the Antinori winery had in determining their choice of the Florentine studio. I think this work is the most significant and mature project built by Archea, and I'm certain that it will remain an icon in the history of European architecture, because it had the ability to place the landscape at the center of our attention and contemporary sensitivity, in addition to achieving the maximum expressive quality of certain obsessions and experiments typical of the Italian studio: from the stairway as a monumental and artistic symbol, to the choice of a few, identifiable materials developed with formal skill, the shaping of the land that, starting from the heart of the earth with the cellars, rises gradually toward the surface to view the existing landscape, framing it with the obvious and decisive horizonal cut. In this work we perceive the tradition of the Italian landscape and innovation, material and function, dialogue between interior and exterior, and absolute quality of the workplaces and those devoted to pleasure. This Tuscan project is the natural prelude to two recent works: the Kiss Bridge at Phú Quốc in Vietnam and the Viola Park, recently completed on the outskirts of Florence. In the former case, we have a unique, paradoxical infrastructure – a bridge that is broken at the center, leaving a gap of just 30 centimeters where individuals on either side can reach across to shake hands or kiss. It is unquestionably a highly symbolic and exceptional monument for a new, important tourist location in the south of that country. For the Viola Park, however, the scale of the landscape wins out over the individual fragments built, and binds them skillfully together, restoring a featureless part of the city that begged to be reunited with the rest of the area.

The works about which we have spoken demonstrate a pride for the built structure and an awareness that certain contexts require bold, ambitious spatial and constructive choices that add personality for a future in which the environmental challenges and the demands of quality in our built environment will be decisive.

All this arises from the necessary and constructive interaction between the clients and the designers, knowing that this first link will expand gradually to the different communities that will inhabit it and transform it, thanks to generous environments capable of welcoming the life force and accepting the demands that will emerge in the coming decades in every metropolis in the world.

All the interviews that follow were conducted by Luca Molinari [**LM**].

ANTINORI NEL CHIANTI CLASSICO WINERY

PIERO ANTINORI

PIERO ANTINORI

September 11th 2024 | A gash in the earth and the innovative construction of a form of landscape that does not offend the surrounding territory but, rather, continues the ideal of the thoughtful construction of a strongly anthropicized and natural location. The interview with Marquis Piero Antinori [**PA**] — Honorary President of Marchesi Antinori SpA — in the midst of the new winery, gives us the idea of building as a responsibility and, at the same time, of caring for the land that nourishes such highly prized vineyards. Before an audience of enthusiasts and wine experts at work on the new harvest, we discuss the role of the Antinori nel Chianti Classico winery as an ice-breaker for eno-gastronomic tourism in Italy, and the importance of architecture for respect of the landscape.

LM It's a great pleasure to be a guest of this extraordinary place, with the winery at our back while we admire the view of the Tuscan countryside all around us. This amazing piece of architecture, born of an incision in the landscape, could only have been imagined by a profoundly intuitive designer, supported by the desires and needs of the client.

I know the long story of this project, which originated as a more invasive plan, later modified following the unexpected proposal of Archea. How did it all start? What were you looking for?

PA The project originated more than 25 years ago because of our need to move from the historical site of the cellar that had become, over the years, inadequate both as regards the size – we had no more room to grow – and for technological reasons.

We found the space we needed on this hill near the village of Bargino and asked various architects to send us their project ideas. The proposal we received from Marco Casamonti and the Archea studio immediately got our attention and we were quite enthusiastic at how well it corresponded to our own vision, both structurally – the layout met our needs exactly – and esthetically.

Our vision was to continue as we had for many centuries, contributing in time to make this landscape unique and exceptionally beautiful.

A countryside is not a product of Mother Nature, who has so generously gifted us with these lovely, rolling hills, alone, but is also a human enterprise in many ways, from an agricultural standpoint – through our plantings of olive trees, the inimitable cypresses that line our avenues, our vineyards – but also from the urban viewpoint, all of which contribute to generate the image of the Tuscan landscape, thanks to the harmonious way in which the built environments have been inserted.

Our desire was to pursue this same approach to the landscape with our project. We wanted to create a work of architecture that would become part of the countryside without ruining it, but at the same time giving it a strong contemporary flavor. This was the basis for the two deep cuts made in the land, connecting the cellar, built into the hillside, with the surrounding landscape.

LM It is what we now define as a landmark. While you were telling us about the genesis of the project, I was thinking about how obvious it is that the landscape is the result of this very complex and fragile relationship between human activities and nature; but it is also obvious that the former have recognized and respected the quality of the latter.

In some ways we could say that it is a project in which protection, tradition and innovation manage to achieve a perfect balance. It think these are the three main values that we also encounter in your history; and by history I mean the history of a family that has always lived according to these values, as well as with a great bond of love for the landscape and this land in particular.

PA I think an important family trait of ours has always been to combine tradition and innovation, because really, I think, a tradition is simply an innovation that turns out well. This winery is the symbolic representation of that unity.

LM How did the project change in the dialogue between you and the architect? Was the first project presented to you similar to what we see now?

PA The project did not change in any substantial way from the first idea; that character that excited us so much remained the same. Some changes were made as the drawings were being prepared, in the sense that the project was a very significant investment for us, and could only be justified in function of the long term.

At first there was also some question as to whether it should be built in its final form, as we had originally thought, or if we should remove some parts, such as the spiral staircase, for example.

Later, however, we gave it our full-throated approval and decided to build it as planned, and in so doing created one of the most characterizing elements of the winery.

LM I'd like to go back to that first period, because I'm interested in understanding the nature of your impression on seeing, for the first time, those two totally unexpected incisions on the hill. By choosing this project you contributed to initiate an architectural season of designer wineries also thanks to this work which is, indeed, a historical work of architecture.

What did you think when you saw those two openings?

PA Like I said at the beginning, it was something that thrilled me immediately because It exactly corresponded to what we had in mind. I never had the slightest doubt that it could be the ideal solution.

LM I understand that the greatest patrons of the art always choose on the basis of their instincts; other factors may enter into the negotiations later, but the first contact with the future project is the one that triggers an immediate emotion and ensures the client that the choice made is the right one.

It does take a certain amount of courage, however, because it is a bold concept, both from the economic standpoint and also from that of the physics of the construction; this, for example, is a work that reinvents the landscape and thereby confirms that architecture is effectively a landscape in itself.

PA Architecture has always reinvented the landscape, enriching it as it did in the previous centuries, with villas, castles, churches and villages: all architecture designed with great artistic talent and knowledge that has contributed to embellish the landscape. I think this work can rightfully claim its place in that line of tradition and culture.

LM It is a form of contemporary coherence. One of the things I love most about this project is the view in cross section. It is surprising because these vaulted rooms in the belly of the earth are where you store the barriques and where all the technical equipment at the service of the cellar and the production of wine are housed. Then, from darkness, we proceed gradually upward toward the light, protected by this great ceiling that cuts across the horizontal view of the landscape. The project continues through a sequence of spaces characterized by very different materials and textures: brick, wood, cor-ten steel…

PA All products of the Tuscan territory: the aging cellar is lined with terracotta from Impruneta, which is a material specific to this zone, and even the parts worked in wood derive from local lumber, the same that is used to produce our barrels.

LM This aspect is important, because it renders the architecture more solid and rooted in the land and region for which it was designed. This is a work of architecture that belongs to the land: the same land that nourishes the vineyards and that is itself part of the architecture.

In twelve years, or perhaps even more, how has this architecture aged? What has it taught you about living in it and experiencing it? What have you discovered that you didn't expect?

PA One of the reasons the project excited me immediately was that it gave me the impression of being timeless, capable of looking modern even centuries from now, beyond the logics of fashion.

At the same time, this work opened new market dynamics, as it awakened a desire on the part of the consumers of our products to know where they came from, how and by whom the wine was produced. A work of such renown as this encouraged the growth of a more cultured wine tourism. They are consumers who are not satisfied with just holding a glass of wine: they want to know what's in the bottle. This work served, I think, as a calling card that gave greater added value to our wines and to the recognizability of our company.

LM So the architecture in some way also strengthened the narrative and the history that lies behind it all. I wonder, when you look at what you have done, if you ever think of adding to it, changing it…

PA I'd say absolutely not, and reiterate the concept I expressed before relative to the fact that I expect this project to age well, like fine wine.

LM We spoke of the landscape, which in some ways you rebuilt. Could you tell me why you feel it is so important for us to take care of the places we transform?

PA At this point, wine is produced just about everywhere in the world, but I think that what distinguishes us and gives us our particular advantage is the fact that, unlike other countries, our history, our culture and our traditions have taught us how to treat the landscape with the necessary care.

LM This particular sensitivity is also present in your wonderful art collection, in which every work confirms this love for a contemporary world, where history and innovation live together naturally.

LOCATION	Bargino, San Casciano Val di Pesa, Florence, Italy [N 43°36'44.838" E11°11'28.93"]
PROGRAM	Winery and cellars, offices, museum, auditorium, restaurant, roadways, plazas, green areas, purification system
DIMENSIONS	Area: 130,000 sqm (32 acres) Built area: 39,700 sqm
CHRONOLOGY	Start of project: 2004; start of works at site: 2007 Completion of works: October 25, 2012
CLIENT	Marchesi Antinori Honorary Chairman Piero Antinori
ARCHITECTURAL PROJECT, INTERIOR DESIGN, FURNISHINGS, GRAPHIC PROJECT AND ART DIRECTION	Archea / Marco Casamonti: Laura Andreini Marco Casamonti Silvia Fabi Giovanni Polazzi
PROJECT COORDINATOR	Francesco Giordani
ARCHITECTURAL PROJECT TEAM	Enrico Ancilli, Niccolò Balestri, Domenico Giovanni Cacciapaglia, Elena Catalano, Marco Gamberi, Valentina Malta, Alice Marzorati, Michelangelo Perrella, Alessandro Riccomi, Gabriele Sestini
GRAPHIC PROJECT TEAM	Elisa Balducci, Sara Castelluccio, Katia Carlucci, Caroline Fuchs, Vitoria Muzi, Mauro Sampaolesi, Lara Tonnicchi
ENGINEERING, COORDINATION GENERAL AND URBAN PROCEDURES ADMINISTRATIVE FUNCTIONS	HYDEA
WORKS MANAGEMENT	Paolo Giustiniani
STRUCTURAL DESIGN	AEI Progetti
DESIGN OF INSTALLATIONS	M&E Management & Engineering
SPECIALIZED DESIGN	Geology: Marco Bastogi; Paolo Canuti Geotechnology: Marco Sacchetti Winemaking equipment: Emex Engineering; Marchesi Antinori
GENERAL CONSTRUCTION COMPANY	Inso
DESIGN OF MUSEUM PORTION	Alessia Antinori
CURATORSHIP OF INSTALLATIONS AND TEMPORARY EXHIBITIONS	Chiara Parisi

The site is surrounded by the unique hills of Chianti Classico, covered with vineyards, half-way between Florence and Siena. A cultured and illuminated customer has made it possible to pursue, through architecture, the enhancement of the landscape and the surroundings as expression of the cultural and social valence of the place where wine is produced. The functional aspects have therefore become an essential part of a design itinerary which centres on the geo-morphological experimentation of a building understood as the most authentic expression of a desired symbiosis and merger between anthropic culture, the work of man, his work environment and the natural environment.
The purpose of the project has therefore been to merge the building and the rural landscape; the production complex appears to be a part of the latter thanks to the roof, which has been turned into a plot of farmland cultivated with vines, interrupted, along the contour lines, by two horizontal cuts which let light into the interior and provide those inside the building with a view of the landscape through the imaginary construction of a diorama. The façade, to use an expression typical of buildings, therefore extends horizontally along the natural slope, paced by the rows of vines which, along with the earth, form its "roof cover". The openings or cuts discreetly reveal the underground interior: one of the office areas, organized like a belvedere above the barricade, and the areas where the wine is produced are arranged along the lower, and the bottling and storage areas along the upper. The secluded heart of the winery, where the wine matures in barrels, conveys, with its darkness and the rhythmic sequence of the terracotta vaults, the sacral dimension of a space which is hidden, not because of any desire to keep it out of sight but to guarantee the ideal thermo-hygrometric conditions for the slow maturing of the product. A reading of the architectural section of the building reveals that the altimetrical arrangement follows both the production process of the grapes which descend (as if by gravity) – from the point of arrival, to the fermentation tanks to the underground barrel vault – and that of the visitors who on the contrary ascend from the parking area to the winery and the vineyards, through the production and display areas from the museum area, the bookshop, the wine tasting areas and the shop to finally reach the floor hosting the grape reception area, the area where vinsanto is aged and the restaurant. The rest of the offices are paced by a sequence of internal court illuminated by circular holes scattered across the vineyard-roof. The materials and technologies evoke the local tradition with simplicity, coherently expressing the theme of studied naturalness, both in the use of terracotta and in the advisability of using the energy produced naturally by the earth to cool and insulate the cellar, creating the ideal climatic conditions for the production of wine.

Marchesi
ANTINORI
NEL CHIANTI CLASSICO

"Our vision was to continue as we had for many centuries, contributing in time to make this landscape unique and exceptionally beautiful." — Piero Antinori

ANTINORI NEL CHIANTI CLASSICO

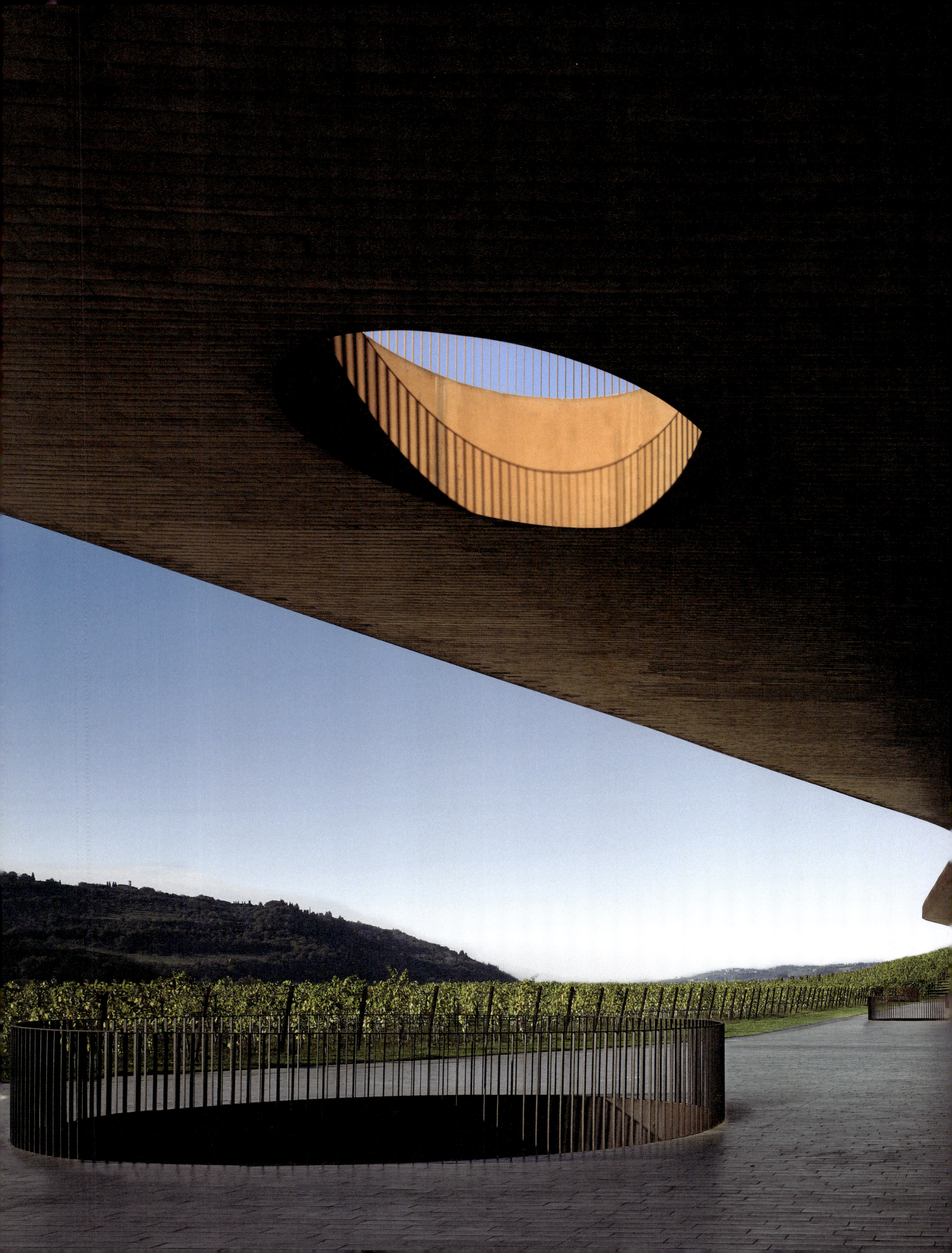

2004 | 2013

"One of the reasons the project excited me immediately was that it gave me the impression of being timeless, capable of looking modern even centuries from now, beyond the logics of fashion."

— Piero Antinori

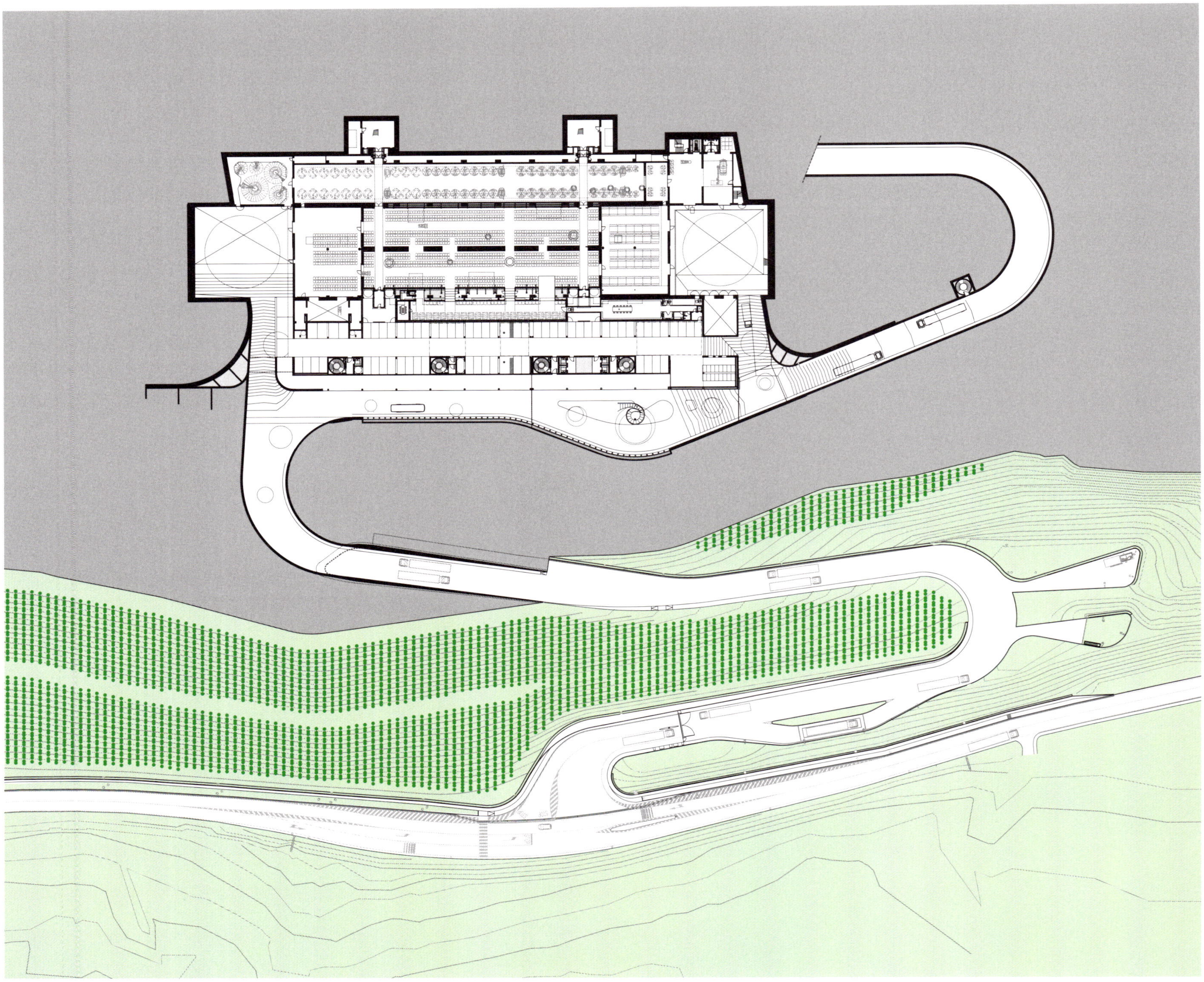

Plan altitude +169.65

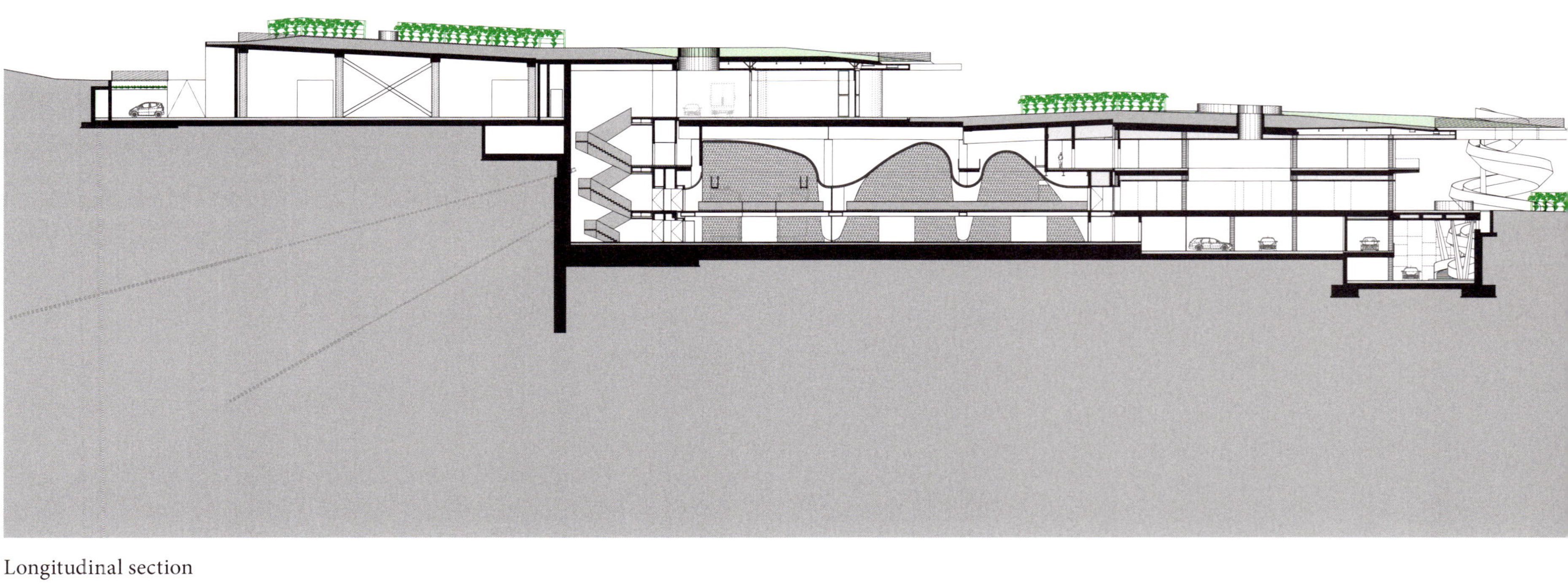

Longitudinal section

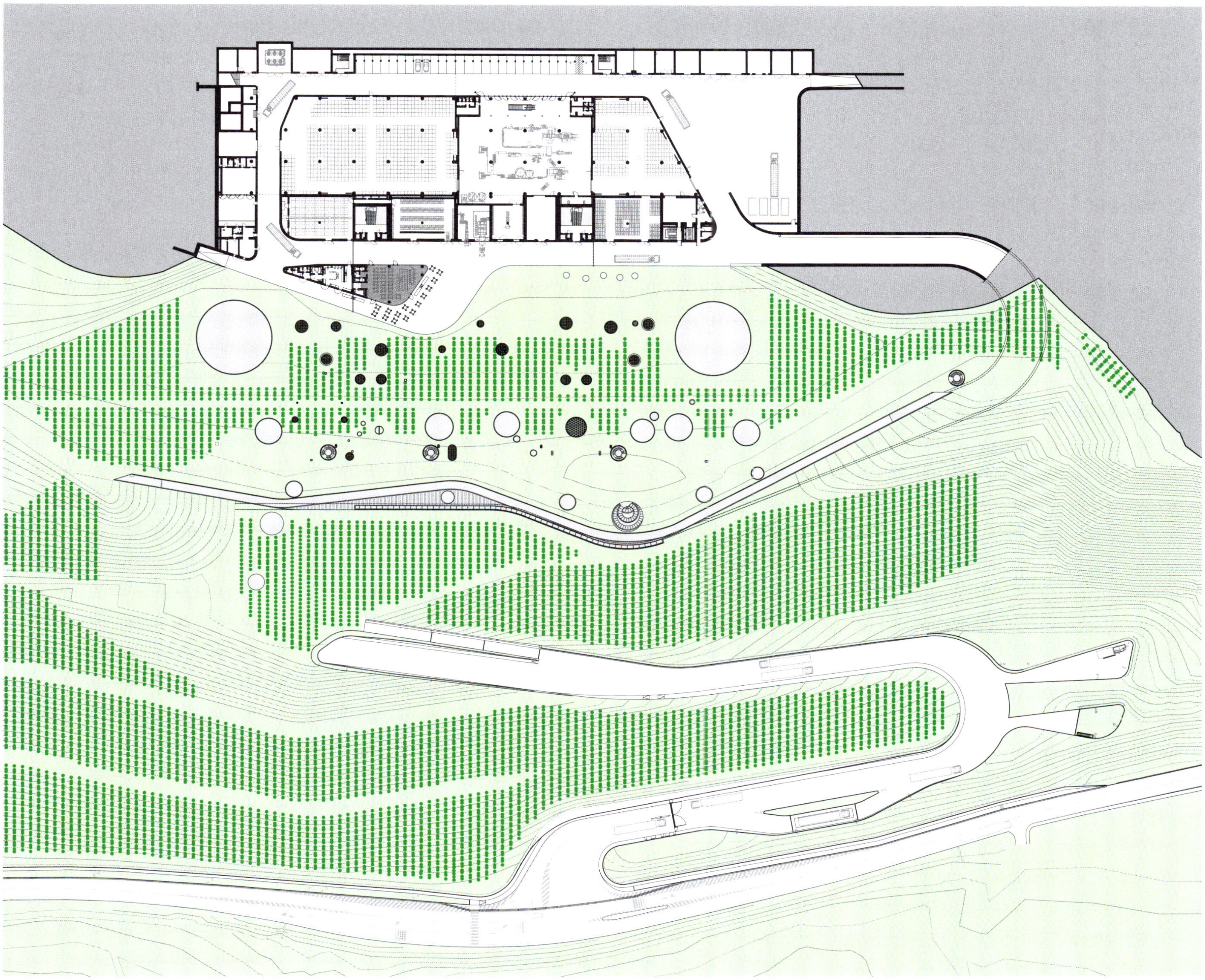

Plan altitude +184.00

0 10 20 50 m

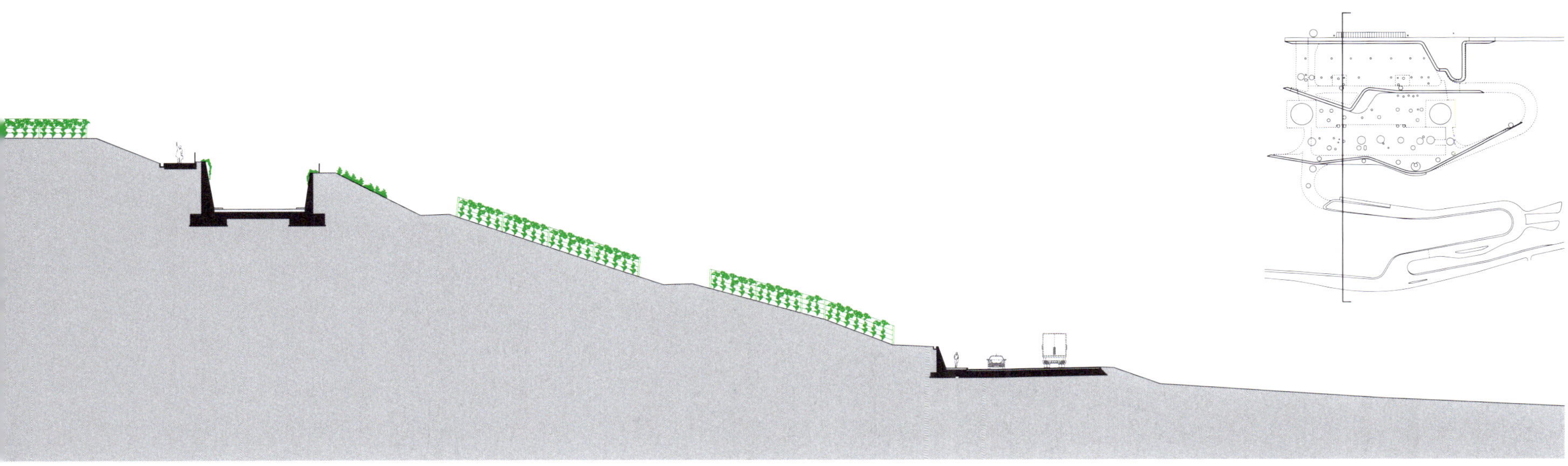

0 5 10 20 m

05.2004 Presentation to the client of the first feasibility study proposing a fully interred building that would restore the old vineyard. This study was developed into a project and later built.

08.2005 Delivery of the detailed plans necessary to obtain the building permit.

04.2007 Construction of a fence around the project area and construction of the cellar section of the plan.

12.2007 First sampling of the vaults for barriques and the wine-fermenting room (in the version as later built) produced with metallic structures on which elements in terracotta would be fastened, using a technique similar to that of ventilated walls, but adapted for this product so as to ensure a specific level of insulation, while keeping within the allotted budget.

03.2008 The worksite is subject to landslides, which necessitates the interruption of works for about a year and a half, during which time a project was drafted for geotechnical consolidation, and the relative architectural variant was designed and approved.

03.2011 Start of construction of the vaults, starting from the section of the wine cellar at the farthest end of the four that would eventually make up the entire system.

11.2011 The consolidation project drafted previously, was entirely built and completed.

09.2011 At this point, with works of impermeabilization of the roofing completed, and the drainage system installed, it was possible to start preparing the land and planting the vineyard that would restore the original landscape.

06.2012 The executive and built project is integrated with the monumental spiral staircase that will complete the system of entrances; at the same time, the foundations are completed at the worksite with the metallic roofing structures that will help to support the 100 tons of steel necessary for the construction of the stairway.

09.2012 Works begin on construction of the stairway; at first, the separate sections take shape, one by one, at the mill, and are then delivered to the worksite and assembled with structural welding. The entire stairway would be completed in time for the inauguration the following month.

10.2012 Inauguration before an audience of citizens and authorities, while the company went ahead with moving out of the old production facilities and offices structures in San Casciano Val di Pesa and into the new ones at Bargino.

218,000 cu. m	total volume of construction
130,000 sqm	lot area, fenced area
8,050 sqm	external roads and parking area
11,700 sqm	internal roads and parking area
522 m	length of underground walkways
380,000 cu. m	earth removed
110,000 cu. m	earth replaced
1780	foundation piles
16.50 m	average length of foundation piles
710	tie rods
27.25 m	average length of tie rods
9,500 sqm	diaphragm area
21,35 m	maximum height of diaphragm
32,358 cu. m	reinforced concrete
3,317,550 kg	steel in bars for reinforced concrete
10,742 sqm	terracotta
60 km	total length of track supporting paneling in terracotta of the vault
1,509,191 kg	metallic structures

ROCCO B. COMMISSO VIOLA PARK

ROCCO COMMISSO

ROCCO COMMISSO

September 25th 2024 | What was once an abandoned area on the outskirts of Florence is now the Viola Park, the largest campus for soccer in Europe, where the design of the landscape features various architectural works with low environmental impact, built in wood and steel, alternating with the playing fields. We meet Rocco Commisso [**RC**] — President of ACF Fiorentina — in one of the new pavilions and our conversation touches on the changing world of soccer, on the need to imagine the Fiorentina team, its ownership, management, players and fans as a community, enlarged to include players of different ages and genders, all living together, and where environmental responsibility and the architecture of the park are important elements for the future of the city.

LM Let's start from the beginning. Some friends told me that this used to be a desolate place, an unofficial garbage dump, before this beautiful Viola Park was built. So, where does the story start?

RC Right! The story begins in July of 2019. We had just bought the Fiorentina Club. When I came to Florence, I scheduled a meeting with Mayor Francesco Casini in Bagno a Ripoli to see this location in case I wanted to do something with it. That was a phenomenal experience for me because I saw a latent beauty that I didn't expect to find so close to Florence. So, I said we have to buy this land.

I hadn't met Marco Casamonti yet, but I knew the first thing we had to do was buy the property. It was in two parts, one connected to the villa and the other to the rest of the acreage. It added up to around 64 acres or 250,000 square meters that we bought within a couple of months. Then we started looking as projects.

LM I think the Viola Park is a new way of looking at sports, not just in Italy, but also in Europe. It is a kind of campus where you not only have the club, but space for families and communities to meet together in this lovely landscape. What was your vision in commissioning this work?

RC Well the main idea is to bring everybody together in one place. We have over twenty teams, between our youth groups and the women's and men's soccer teams playing all over the metropolitan area of Florence. My vision was to have everybody playing and training at the same place. Marco's design enabled us to accomplished this: we have these beautiful buildings devoted to all the needs of the teams playing here; we have the building for the first team, the women, the men, and another one for the kids. Every day, the youth teams come to train in the splendid complex: a total of about 2,500 between children just starting to play and older talent.

We put it all together, little by little, thanks to Marco Casamonti. He was definitely the perfect architect to design these phenomenal structures.

I changed very few things, like the pillars, for example. At the outset, the structure was supported by wooden pillars, and I didn't like them very much. So, Marco came up with the idea of using "V" shaped pillars; we liked it, and moved forward with this idea.

LM What impresses me is the way the architecture harmonizes with the landscape, especially in relation to the fact that you made use of some old buildings, regenerating them. It's a process of regeneration that cleverly merges the architecture and landscape and gives this part of the city a totally new look.

RC Right! This will be here forever; I'm sure I'll be dead, and this will still be alive. So, it's an addition to the beauty of Florence. We don't have a stadium yet, because the existing one is old. They are trying to remodel it now.

But we have the Viola Park. It cost a lot of money, but I think my wife and my family agree with me and we are all very happy we managed to complete it. The work was done very quickly, you know, because we only met with the Mayor in 2019, so in just two years, we had it almost finished!

LM Despite the pandemic…

RC … and the war in Ukraine! We got clobbered on construction costs, because that's where the steel came from. All the prices went up and it was a mess, but we went ahead and did it.

LM Does your campus fit well with the idea of Fiorentina? First, you acquired the Fiorentina Club, which has a long history. Soccer has changed a lot in the last 30 years, and most of the big clubs have invested in new stadiums or new centers where the idea is no longer to have single-function facilities like a stadium, but investing in more multi-function sports centers, open to different communities at different times of day and different seasons. These sports centers thus become an all-round part of the city. How do you feel that the Viola Park fits with the values of the Club?

RC We have events here. We don't just play soccer here; when Fiorentina plays away, there is an auditorium at the Viola Park where can people come and watch the game on television. When local businessmen want to have an event for their companies, they can have it here. If you take a walk around, we have an events pavilion that can accommodate 500 people. We have a complex with 75 rooms where the women's, children's and men's teams can rest. So, it is a multi-functional center, not just for the first team players and coaching staff…

LM I've heard that there are places where kids can do their homework, which is really important for the younger players…

RC Yes, we have study rooms where the kids are followed by adults to ensure they keep up with their schoolwork and studies… It's almost a 24-hour affair for them: they get up in the morning and go to school, and then they come back here, study and practice. We also have external events. It's a costly place to manage every single day of the year. We hope these events will bring us some extra revenue to help us subsidize…

LM It's part of the overall business plan…

RC The other thing I want to say – and I think Marco should get the credit for that – is that we just bought another 50,000 square meters for parking. We came here, and they promised us they would give us the parking area, but we got nothing. The city was supposed to bring the tram out here to an annexed parking area, which would have facilitated our fans to come here. In the end, we had to go out and buy some additional land for parking.

Today, I'm pretty sure the Viola Park is the largest facility of its kind in Italy and Europe. In America, football, basketball, soccer and baseball teams get young players from colleges and universities, so they don't need to have something like this. There is no such thing as having more than 2 or 3 fields.

LM The idea of sports at the university is very strong, based on your American experience. Over there, education, teaching, community, and sports are all part of the same experience, and completely overlap.

RC I went to Columbia University, where we have 34 men's and women's teams that play throughout the year. Outdoor sports like hockey, lacrosse, football, baseball, softball, or soccer are all played at Baker Field. This site, Viola Park, is twice the size of Baker Field.

LM It's an open landscape, which impressed me right the first. It's important to note here that this was not just an architectural project, but a landscape project as well: playing in the open requires you to take account of sustainability, circularity, and the idea of ecology, which is very contemporary and necessary. I think the Viola Park has become a kind of focus project for the city of Florence and its future overall, hasn't it?

RC I agree. We did everything to ensure that this beautiful piece of land can thrive forever. We built a lake, and I don't know many flowers, trees, and shrubs we've planted here.

Everyone who works here – the staff, the players and everybody else – is proud and happy to work here.

LM This was one of my questions because Viola Park opened a year ago, and so you have had chance to see how the different communities react to it: not just the players, but the fans, the local communities, and other people… What sorts of comments and reactions impressed you most, in terms of feedback?

RC Well, I've been more than impressed by many things – some have even moved me to tears. In October of last year, when we had the grand opening, that was one, and it was spectacular. I didn't know what they would do, but we spent the money, and they brought everybody here, and all our fans came… As I said before, all the people who have been in any way involved with this project, from me and my wife to my family and my staff on, are just immensely proud and happy. Marco Casamonti did all this by bringing the Viola Park to life…

LM Architecture is always a matter of trust in the future because, as they say, you plant a tree today, which will give shade after many years, to the next generation. Without that vision of the future, we couldn't have architecture. You know exactly what it means to invest in the future, so you know what a critical investment this is for the future generation, the Club, and so on…

Fiorentina is so close to its fans and to the city of Florence; I mean, in Florence, any discussion of soccer ends up being about Fiorentina.

RC It's not a big city like Milan, Rome, or Naples, but we have very loyal fans. It's a one-club city. We work to play winning games for our fans and bring some trophies home whenever we can.

LM My last question is related to architecture. This new building, built of steel and wood, is fully sustainable architecture; it is a kind of zero-impact building. That means we're doing something that has a positive environmental impact on the context. Today, it's very important to invest in technologies and materials that are eco-friendly…

RC Marco could answer better than me on this point. As much as possible, we tried to do the right thing by not importing any extraneous materials to this land…

LM You built a dream, and now what you built is part of this community. What do you expect from the Viola Park in the future?

RC We expect to grow a lot of champions here! The idea is to recruit and train young players, as many as possible, in the hope that they will eventually increase the revenues of the Viola Park by playing on the Fiorentina team…

LM Well, you've certainly got a beautiful place to train them and give them a positive outlook…

RC I just know that in our case, people want to stay with Fiorentina, play for Fiorentina, and come to Viola Park. They can't feel that way about another club… So that's a competitive advantage we have…

LOCATION	Bagno a Ripoli, Florence, Italy [N 43°45'27.879" E 11°19'12.829"]
PROGRAM	Sports center, small stadium, offices, cafeteria, medical center, TV studio, conference and events hall, chapel
DIMENSIONS	Area: 26,000 sqm (64 acres) Built area: 29,000 sqm
CHRONOLOGY	Area purchase, permits and project: October 2019-March 2021 Works at site: April 2021-September 2023
CLIENT	ACF Fiorentina Srl President Rocco B. Commisso
ARCHITECTURAL PROJECT, AND ART DIRECTION	Archea / Marco Casamonti: Laura Andreini Marco Casamonti Silvia Fabi Giovanni Polazzi
CONSULTANTS	Riccardo Bartoloni Loris Macci Giampiero Pugliese
PROJECT COORDINATOR	Francesco Dall'Ò
WORKS MANAGEMENT	Alvise Tassi
ON SITE SUPERVISION	Marco Infanti, Matilde Parravicini, Fabio Fanello
ARCHITECTURAL PROJECT TEAM	Lorenzo Albizzi, Pasquale De Lucia, Salvatore Franciosa, Marco Gamberi, Anna Luongo, Antonio Mancuso, Laura Martucciello, Valentina Raggi
STRUCTURAL DESIGN	GPA Partners
DESIGN OF INSTALLATIONS AND FIRE PROTECTION	GPA Energy
SPECIALIZED DESIGN	Geology: Geo Eco Progetti Hydraulics: West System Glazed partitions: Paolo Mariottoni
GENERAL CONSTRUCTION COMPANY	Nigro & C. Costruzioni Srl
PLAYING FIELDS AND ORNAMENTAL PLANTINGS	Rappo Srl Vannucci Piante
HYBRID/SYNTHETIC GRASS FOR SPORTS FACILITIES	Limonta Sport Spa

FIORENTINA STORE

The project for the Rocco B. Commisso Viola Park came about in answer to the desire of the President of Florence's soccer team, Fiorentina, to create something unique, original and exceptional as regards both programming and architecture. The task was certainly facilitated by the beauty of the site, located in one of the most prestigious environmental settings in the Arno valley south of Florence, in the town of Bagno a Ripoli.
In addition to its landscape and environmental value, evidenced by the limitations of a protected zone, based on its significance from the historical and archeological standpoint, as still today it bears the traces and remains of the ancient Roman centuriation.
These traces are clearly visible in the design of the original agrarian layout, and are reflected in the project through the consequent positioning of the playing fields, coinciding with the typical north-south arrangement of the fields, perpendicular and parallel to the line of the Arno and on the upstream side, parallel to the line of the adjacent hills. This crisscross pattern of lines symbolically designs a huge letter "V" on the terrain, at the tip of which is an artificial hill where a chapel, dedicated to St. Catherine, has been erected, along with the events pavilion, the true heart of the sports center.
As regards the rest of the layout, the various pavilions are located near the sections served by municipal utilities, while the events pavilion, representing the central nucleus of the project, is practically invisible, completely hidden from view by the grass.
If the sports center represents the union of different genders and generations, because men, women, teenagers and young children all live and work there, it also establishes a link, between city and country, a sort of in-between space dividing the dense urban community from the precious belt of foothills around Florence.
Every building has a basement area where equipment, changing rooms and rest rooms are located. In the case of the first team, this level is completely devoted to the medical center, swimming pools and spa center, while the gym and changing rooms are located on the ground floor.
On the upper floors, the spaces are used in various ways, depending on the building: some buildings contain offices and others have bedrooms for the players. In this way, all the structures remain low to the ground, coherent with the surrounding architecture. Each building has a steel frame, and is designed with an innovative system of façades using with uprights and beams in wood, and closures in aluminum and glass.
The roofing, also in steel, creates a large overhang that, in addition to providing shade for the windows underneath, serves to collect rainwater that is channeled through a pipeline and used to irrigate the playing fields. A final observation concerns the overall color scheme of the project with the use of shades of brown and green that blend perfectly with the natural surroundings.

"People want to stay with Fiorentina, play for Fiorentina, and come to Viola Park. They can't feel that way about another club… So that's a competitive advantage we have…" — Rocco Commisso

"Every day, the youth teams come to train in the splendid complex: a total of about 2,500 between children just starting to play and older talent."
— Rocco Commisso

ROCCO B. COMMISSO VIOLA PARK

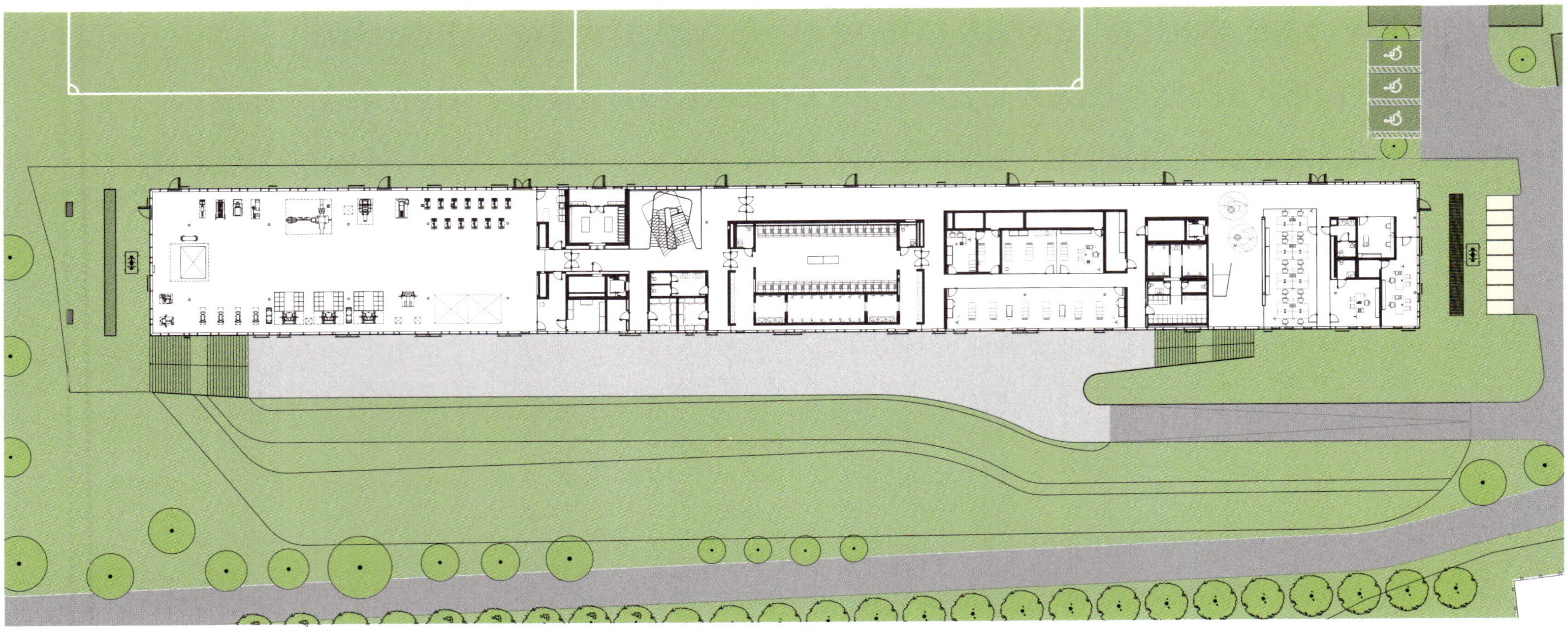

First team pavilion, plan L0

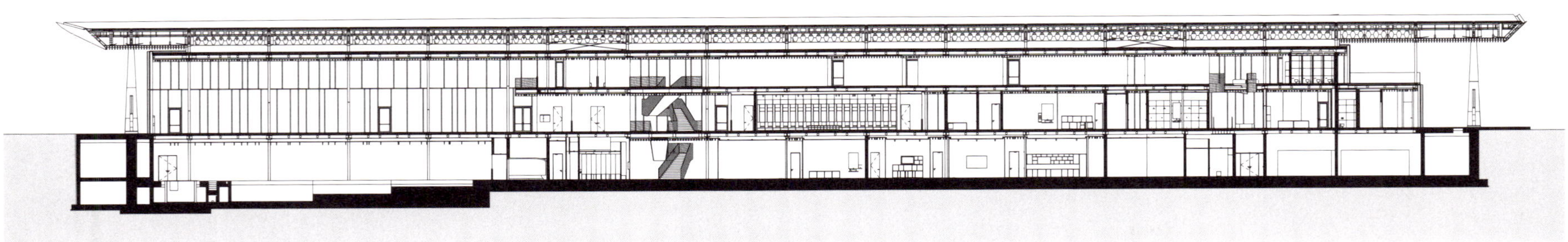

First team pavilion, longitudinal section

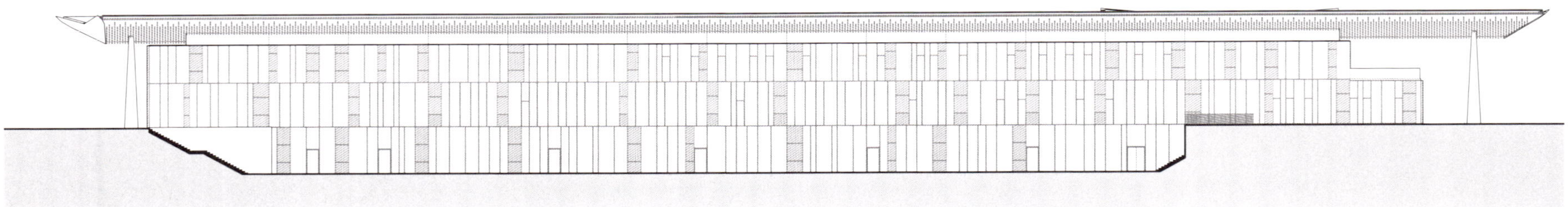

First team pavilion, south-east elevation

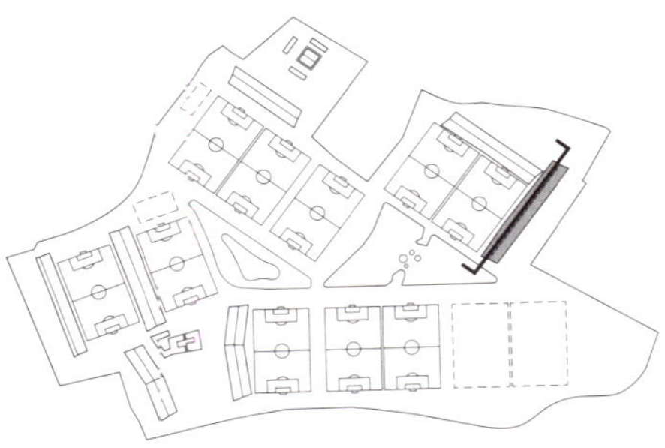

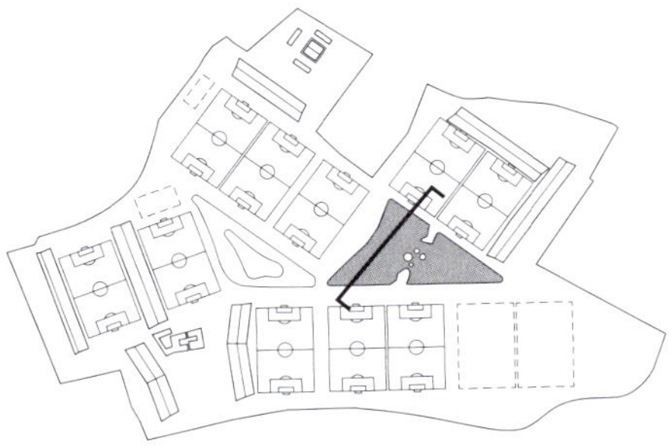

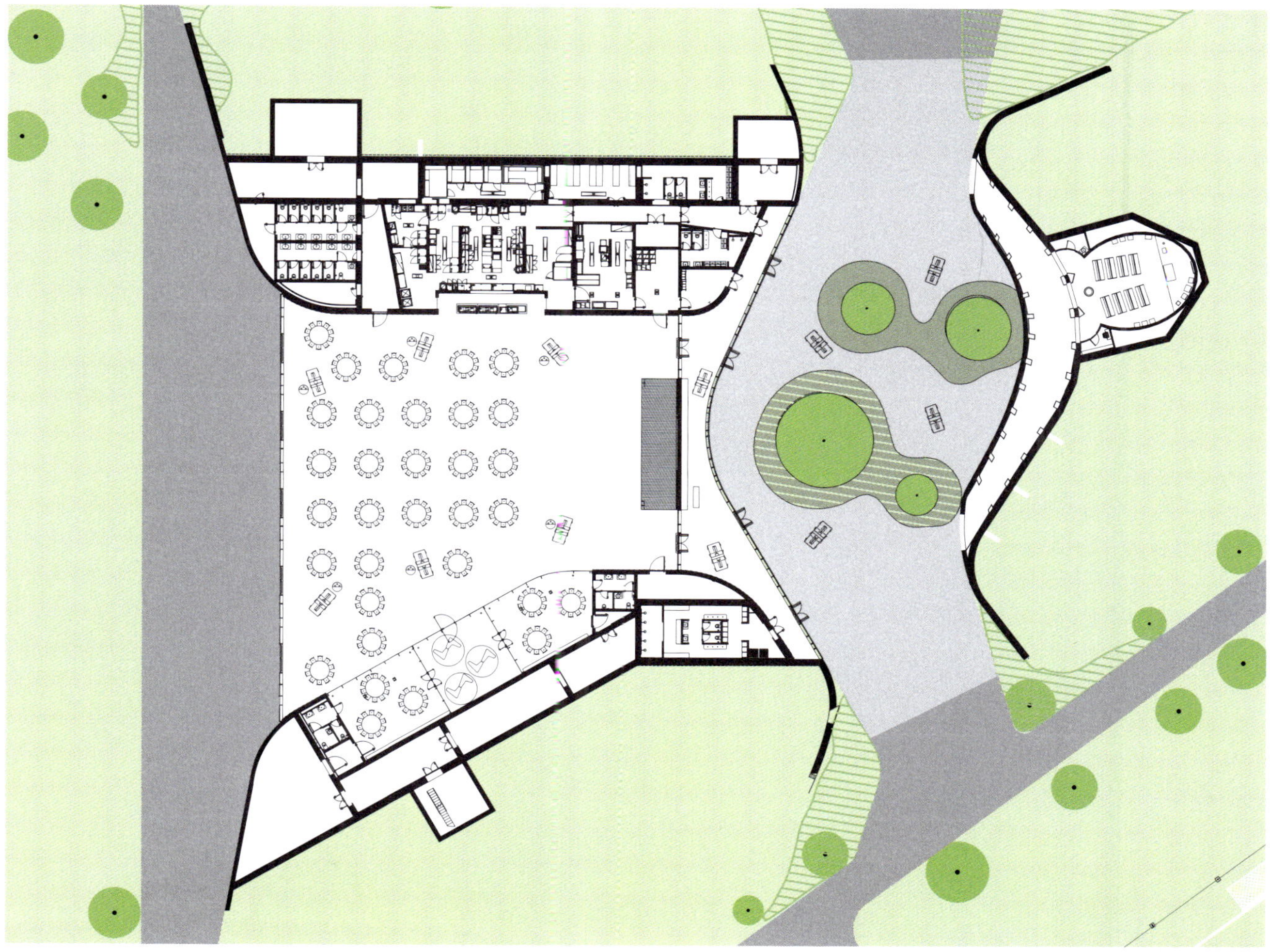

Events pavilion, plan L0

0 5 10 20 m

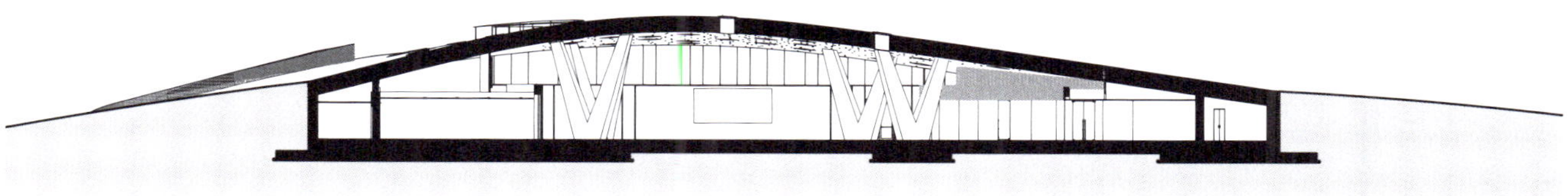

Events pavilion, cross section

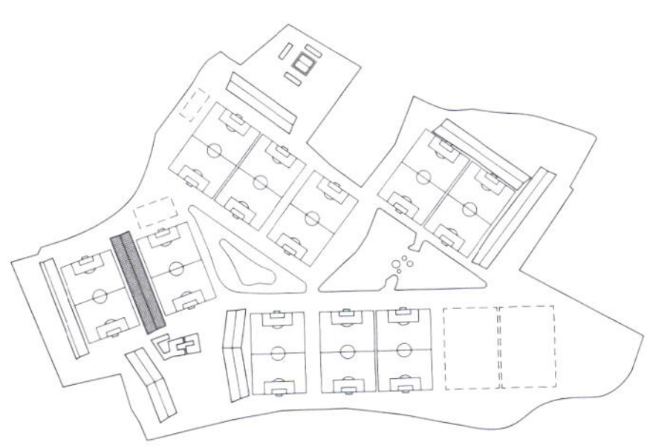

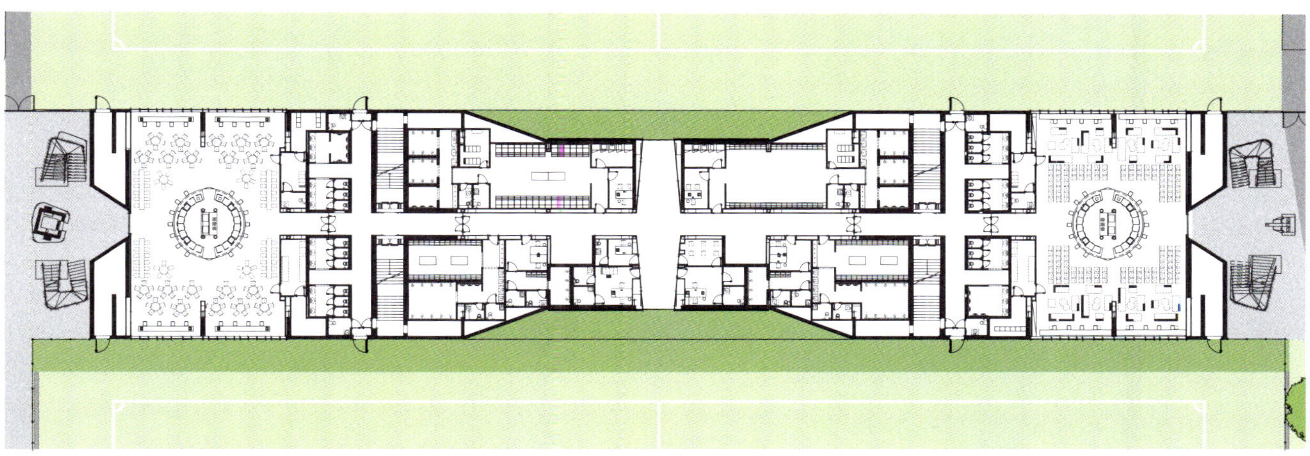

Il Giglio café, Maglia Viola café, plan L0

0 5 10 20 m

06.06.2019 Rocco B. Commisso, founder of the telecommunications company Mediacom Communications Corporation and owner of the American men's soccer team, New York Cosmos, acquires the Italian men's soccer team ACF Fiorentina.

10.09.2019 Fiorentina acquires two adjacent properties in the municipality of Bagno a Ripoli, for a total of about 64 acres of land and a mid-18th century farmhouse with various annexed structures. It is the first property asset owned by the Viola team.

10.26.2020 About a year after purchasing the property, the city council approves the plan to build a new sports center consisting of 10 playing fields, 2 small stadiums, 29,000 square meters of buildings including 12 pavilions and a park with more than 1,000 trees and an artificial lake.

03.11.2021 The first building permits are issued for the Youth pavilion that will be occupied by the young players from beginners to seniors on the youth teams. The basement level contains the changing rooms and service areas, with the gym and technical area on the ground floor. The first floor houses the dining area, study hall and rooms for about 50 athletes.

11.22.2021 Preparation of the playing fields and ornamental plantings. The worksite gets under way with the construction of the playing fields in natural grass – in regulation size – for the women's soccer sector.

05.30.2022 At the conclusion of archeological digs initiated in September 2020, more than 170 tombs from the Etruscan and Roman eras were found, analyzed and catalogued near an ancient Roman cobblestone road.

06.12.2022 Furnishing of the interiors begins. 75 bedrooms, 28 changing rooms, 4 gyms, 67 offices and 19 meeting rooms are furnished. Specialized equipment is installed in 5 industrial kitchens, a medical center and a spa, as well as three hairdresser stations.

02.05.2023 External works of connection to urban utilities such as aqueduct and sewer systems, public works like the construction of bike and pedestrian pathways, as well as on and off ramps to the main highway, SP 34.

07.12.2023 Lodging of the 1st visiting men's team at the beginning of the 2023-24 season.

09.02.2023 Dedication of the chapel in the sports center to St. Catherine of Siena. The bishop of Florence, Cardinal Betori, performs the ceremony.

09.29.2023 Habitability permit issued for the sports installation at the Curva Fiesole Stadium with 3,000 seats approved for the UEFA 2nd Category competitions on natural grass and the Davide Astori Stadium with 1,500 seats and hybrid ground-cover.

10.11.2023 General inauguration of the Rocco B. Commisso Viola Park sports center with Carlo Conti emceeing the evening: 3,000 fans and guests, music and the greetings of the historic football team, fireworks and a 3D drone performance.

05.06.2024 Dedication of the historic 18th century farmhouse to the former General Director, Giuseppe Barone, known to everyone as Joe, who died unexpectedly on March 19 of this year.

1,000 trees

12 pavilions

29,000 sqm built area

2 small stadiums

10 soccer teams

75 bedrooms

67 offices

INA

HAND PRODUCTION BUILDING

SALVATORE FERRAGAMO FACTORY

FERRUCCIO FERRAGAMO

FERRUCCIO FERRAGAMO

July 11th 2024 | The classical Ferragamo "Gancini" logo distinguishes the design of the new factory for production of limited series footwear built near Florence. It is a place where craftsmanship, tradition and innovation thrive together in spaces linked to the history of one of the most prestigious fashion brands in the world. We meet Ferruccio Ferragamo [**FF**] — Former President of Salvatore Ferragamo SpA — at Il Borro, an estate which prides itself on the excellence of its hospitality and cuisine, in the heart of the Tuscan countryside, to discuss the future, regeneration, happy workplaces and the importance of building "artfully" for Italian culture.

LM It's a pleasure to be here with you, enjoying this incredible view we share worldwide. Let's start with this old building, originally a warehouse, which was utterly reimagined and turned into a place of excellence and memory. This dual aspect fascinates me because it reflects what a contemporary factory can be. What inspired this project?

FF This building was created since the space of the shoe factory, dedicated to the ideation of prototypes, needed to be expanded. These models are often inspired by the shoes created sixty, seventy, eighty years ago by my father or my sister Fiamma, preserved in our archive. We thought it was important to make our customers understand the process that drives the production of our shoes.

And it is where Marco Casamonti takes scene, who made every effort to design an architecture, an aerial walkway stretched over the existing assembly line, or as we say in jargon Manovia. In this way, it was possible to show all the stages of production of these special shoes, which in some cases develop creative ideas that were born decades ago.

Marco made us happy because with this project we could invite many people who – by this aerial path – were able to comprehend how much work goes into the creation of a single shoe.

LM One of the intriguing aspects of this project is that it allows you to see the artisans – who are truly artists – working in the same space alongside a wooden wall that resembles a Ceroli sculpture – displaying mockups of all the shoes.

In a single view, you can see both the archive's memory and the work of those using it to recreate and transform these designs today. Let's say it's a visually significant experience.

FF Another critical point is that the aerial walkway connects to the archive where, thanks to my sister Fiamma, all the shoes and models designed by my father are stored. He would study the client and, based on their personality, create a shoe going beyond the concept of just doing a "made to measure" project. This always resulted in maximum customer satisfaction. We have about 14,000 shoe models from my father's career in the archive. The archive does not only preserve shoes, but bags, clothes, silk prints, documents, photographs, videos. It is the safe of the company, where our heritage is preserved. Casamonti thought of a modular space that would accommodate products and documents according to their specificity: compactable cabinets, which create compressible corridors, save space and slide on tracks according to the use. There is also an area for the library, for consulting materials and telling how important the study of fit and feet was for Ferragamo shoes: a job that my father started a long time ago when he was in California and that after him was carried on by the company, transferring his teachings to the production made by machines.

LM The archive holds fourteen thousand shoes which are like portraits of people, in a way… the archive can be imagined like a gallery. I find it amazing that a contemporary factory can integrate an innovative production system that actively engages with memory and a living archive. These elements combine to define a great Italian company like Ferragamo, blending tradition and innovation. The factory and its architecture embody these values.

FF Indeed, the production and reproduction of shoe models inspire everything we do beyond shoes.

LM The red ribbon reminded me of a signature element of the Ferragamo brand: a catwalk. This red steel architectural piece is beautiful and seems weightless as it floats above.

How do the artisans perceive this space? They must have been used to working a very different environment. What were their reactions to this change?

FF The space's design has enhanced the well-being of those working there. I've seen great appreciation from our team. We are fortunate to have wonderful people with us, whom I have always valued, and this project helps them feel even more involved.

LM They are part of a story, your story…

FF Yes, and I think it's essential for everyone to feel they've contributed to a shared achievement.

LM The story transcends the company and becomes part of Italian heritage. Another interesting point is that this project isn't a new factory but the renovation of an existing one. It's about regeneration, a very contemporary theme: reusing what we have instead of building new. You worked on the facade, the interior, and the garden…

FF Yes, we created a green space for leisure time; in front of this area, there's a new warehouse updated with contemporary technology and logic compared to the historic one. Even in this space, we aimed to balance tradition and innovation.

LM Reusing the Ferragamo logo as a decorative element in the garden is a fun way to tell your story.

FF Our "Gancini" logo is visible from above when landing at Peretola…

LM How was it working with Marco Casamonti and Archea? You came up with ideas, and Marco likely responded with even more creativity. How was the collaboration?

FF It was wonderful because we would tentatively suggest our ideas, and Marco always returned to us with ten more ideas and concepts. It was a fantastic collaboration. He has an incredible creative flow and delves deeply into the subject, asking questions that might initially seem unrelated to architecture.

LM This is interesting because I've seen that Ferragamo's identity elements have become seats, green features in the garden, and the red walkway. It's like he enlarged small objects, creating an unexpected effect.

FF Marco is very thorough in his work; he wants to understand everything clearly…

LM I'll close this interview with an almost obvious but important question. Here, we see a great Italian company and an Italian architecture firm collaborating, both producing for the world. You're reinterpreting "Made in Italy" or "Italianness". What makes us special is that we don't just look in the mirror, but constantly renew our image. For instance, you've regenerated a factory, blending identity, work, and memory. This is a way of being Italian in the world. What's your view on the future development of these values?

FF Italians have much to express, even if they communicate less than others who might not have as much to offer. There's a natural evolution in our way of working and thinking. We're lucky to be a country rich in art and inspiration. In 1927, my father returned to Italy from the United States, where he had emigrated in 1914 – he was born in 1898 – partly out of nostalgia but mainly for inspiration, as he wrote in his book. My parents were from Irpinia, but my father chose Florence for its beauty and architecture. I believe all Italians have an inherent awareness and appreciation of beauty and the responsibility to transfer this legacy into the future.

LM This reflects into the art of craftsmanship. In your factory, the “artisanal” way of working stands in a contemporary frame; it’s so nice to see a modern business that preserves age-old skills and craftsmanship.

FF What you are saying is very true; we have been in this factory since 1966. It was once an uncultivated area, and various buildings were gradually adapted and modified. So much has changed since 1966, but we are still here.

LOCATION	Florence, Italy [N 43°48'14.158" E 11°10'44.276"]
PROGRAM	Production facilities building, technical offices
DIMENSIONS	Built area: 5,934 sqm Outdoor areas: 11,000 sqm
CHRONOLOGY	2019–2021
CLIENT	Salvatore Ferragamo Spa
ARCHITECTURAL PROJECT, AND ART DIRECTION	Archea / Marco Casamonti: Laura Andreini Marco Casamonti Silvia Fabi Giovanni Polazzi
PROJECT COORDINATOR	Giovanni Cinquini
ARCHITECTURAL PROJECT TEAM	Valerio Recchioni, Carlotta Roccatagliata
WORKS MANAGEMENT	Massimiliano Cecconi
STRUCTURAL DESIGN	GPA Partners
DESIGN OF INSTALLATIONS AND FIRE PROTECTION	GPA Energy
GENERAL CONSTRUCTION COMPANY	Nigro & C. Costruzioni Srl

Sophisticated renovation and refurbishment work distinguish this building, a project for one of the most important fashion houses in Italian history, Salvatore Ferragamo. The project involved the reorganization and expansion of the old structure of the factory located in Florence: the building, once used as a warehouse, now houses the operations and technical studios of the designers.
The main challenge was to combine the varying working needs dictated by a range of different operating methods, and putting them together in a single place.
The factory, from an anonymous volume, strives to become a work of architecture representative of the brand, as well as transform from what was previously a closed boundary, into an open space, welcome to visitors, and with green spaces in front of the building.
The protagonist of the intervention is an internal suspended walkway, a Red Ferragamo ribbon, placed in the center of the production area on the ground floor, inside a completely black box. Here, there is the iconic bow shape, in reference to one of the historical symbols of the fashion house. The long distribution corridor is a link with the brand's history: thousands of wooden shoe shapes are hung, including some original pieces used to make the elegant shoes of stars – Sophia Loren, Greta Garbo, Marilyn Monroe – all made clearly visible thanks to the surrounding glass walls.
The second floor is completely dedicated to the historical archive of the brand and to the exhibition of the numerous works of art commissioned over time by the company to a range of artists. Volumes, lights, rounded and enveloping shapes characterize the project, providing a clear reference to the colors and the world of fashion, of which Salvatore Ferragamo has always been at the forefront.

HAND PRODUCTION BUILDING

"Another critical point is that the aerial walkway connects to the archive where, thanks to my sister Fiamma, all the shoes and models designed by my father are stored." — Ferruccio Ferragamo

HAND PRODUCTION BUILDING

“The space’s design has enhanced the well-being of those working there. I’ve seen great appreciation from our team.”
— Ferruccio Ferragamo

HAND PRODUCTION BUILDING

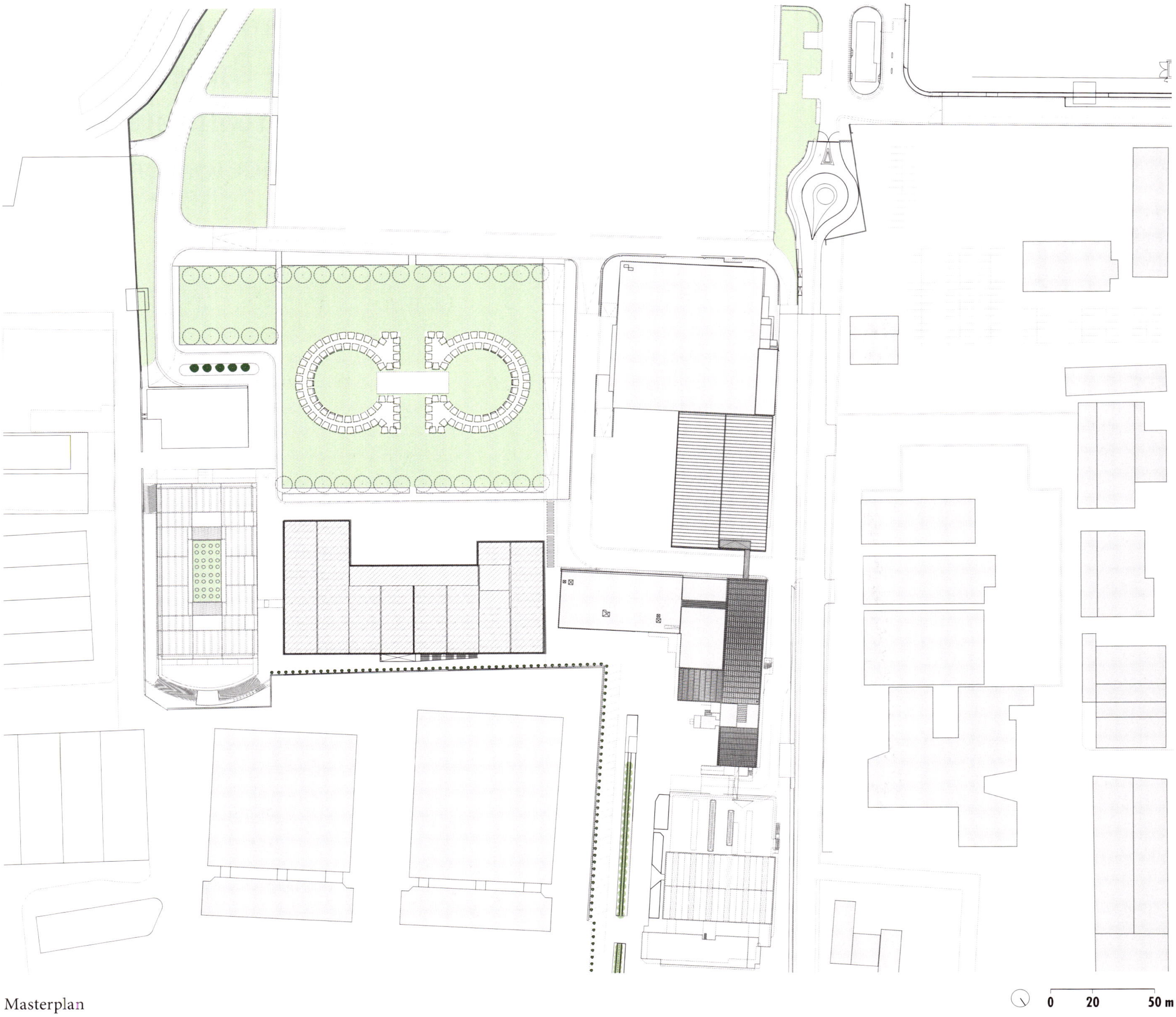

Masterplan

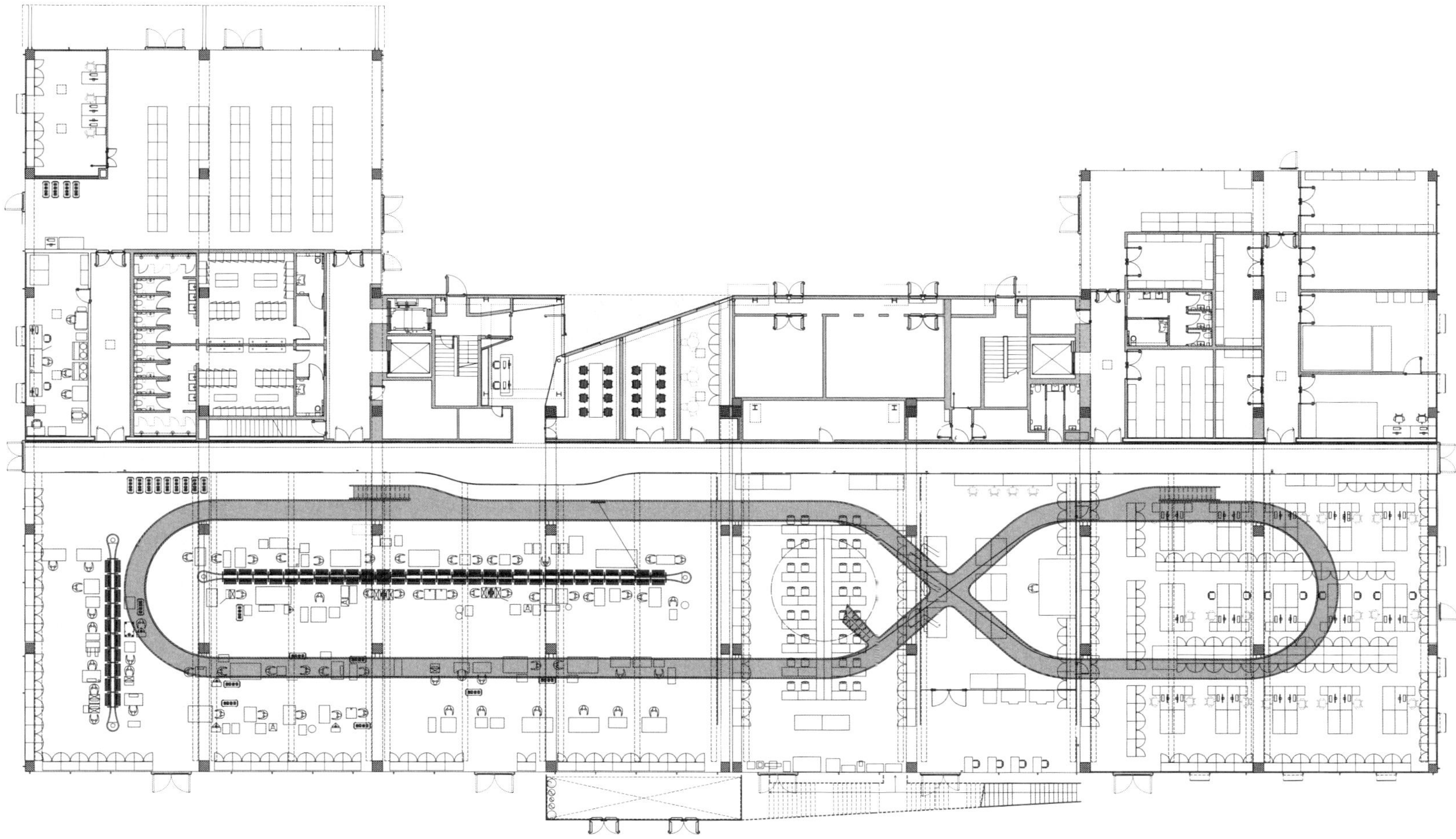

Plan L0

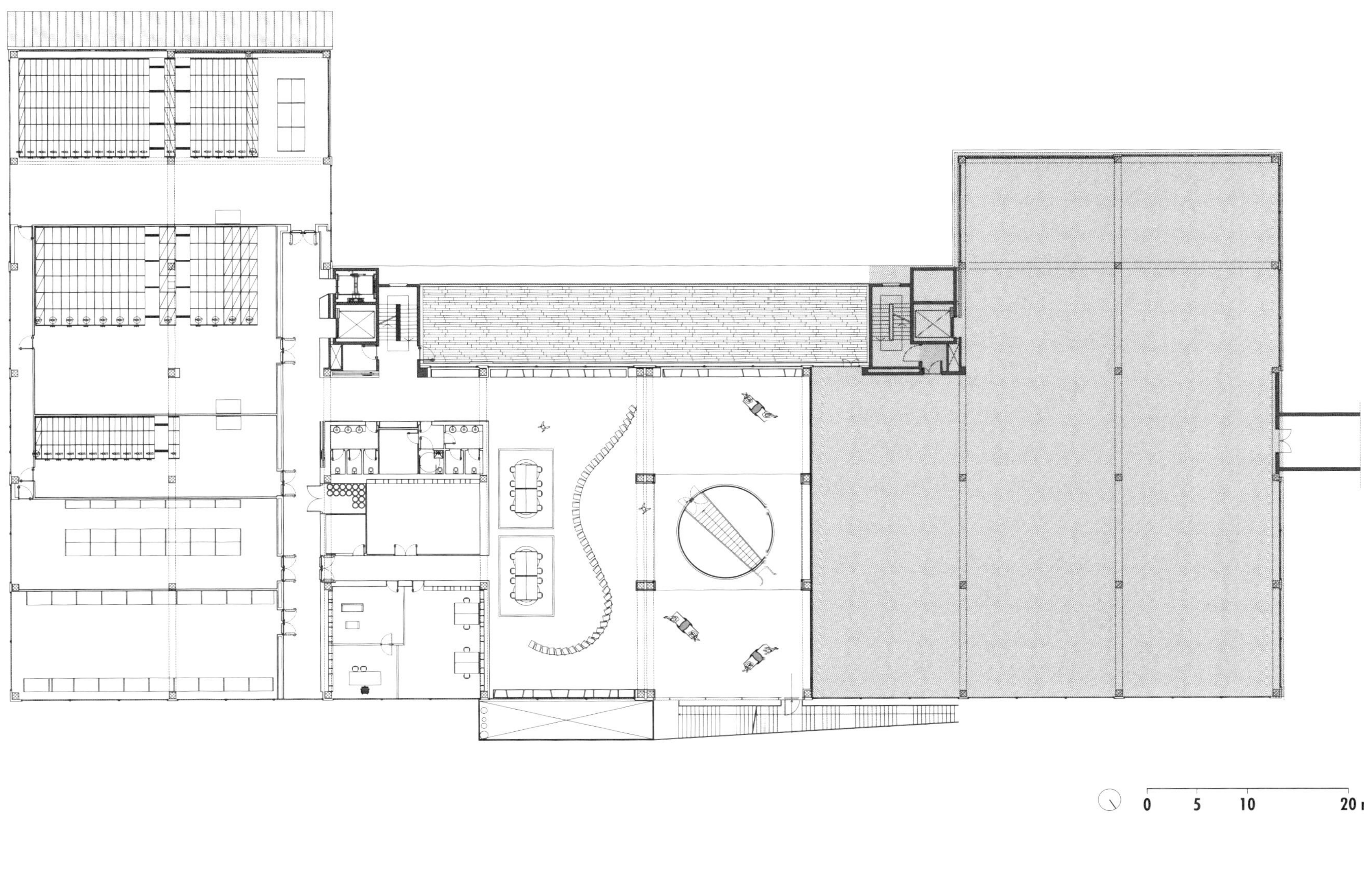

Plan L1

HAND PRODUCTION BUILDING

02.2019 Presentation to the Ferragamo family of the first concept of the project which consisted of combining in a single building both production and technical offices connected to the factory business, allowing them to coexist and interact comfortably while giving brand identity to an otherwise anonymous factory setting lacking any architectural value.

05.2019 After acceptance by the client of the project proposal, while the early stages of work stages were already underway (demolition and construction), the studio put together the executive project for all the interior and exterior works, including the new entrance and the completed custom interior, remaining faithful to the original design concept presented.

07.15.2019 Installation of the "overhead catwalk": an iconic element extending over the production zone that would allow guests and/or supervisors to observe the production process without interfering with the activity going on below.
The design of the catwalk echoes the iconic style themes of Ferragamo fashion shows both in the shapes and in the colors.

08.10.2019 Works of assembly and installation are completed for all the glass elements, both interior and exterior. All the dividing walls between the offices and production zones are glassed, so as to permit a visual permeability of the entire production department. The glass cladding on the outside makes the workspace very luminous and offers a view of the new park in front of the production plant.

08.20.2019 Assembly and installation is completed with regard to the exhibition wall in oak wood left natural, displaying thousands of shoe forms, including original pieces used to produce elegant footwear for Sophia Loren, Greta Garbo and Marilyn Monroe, clearly visible thanks to the fully transparent glass walls, which are a direct reference to the history of the brand.

09.01.2019 On the return of the Ferragamo workers from their summer vacation, the assembly line and all the production zones were complete and functioning, and they can resume working normally.

10.10.2019 The characterizing element of the main entrance to the building is completed, as are all the offices, the warehouses and the zone on the upper floor reserved for the company's museum.

10.15.2019 Inauguration of the entire structure as regards both the production zone and the annexed offices, plus the museum area, the new reception area and the elevated catwalk for visitors.

6,000 sqm worksite area

11,000 sqm external park

1,500 sqm glassed area (interior walls)

800 sqm glassed area (exterior cladding)

1,500 hanging shoe form models

HAND PRODUCTION BUILDING

EDI RAMA

September 16th 2024 | We meet Edi Rama [**ER**] — Prime Minister of Albania — at the Albanian national stadium late in the evening. Despite the hour, the plaza around this monument is filled with people out for a walk, or sitting in the many cafés that surround it. Where once there was darkness and insecurity, now the city is rising again, and the stadium has become one of the symbols of this change. We talk with Edi Rama about his visions for the future of Tirana and of Albania, thanks to the contributions of contemporary architecture and art which have enabled the capital of the country to experience a rebirth and become an immense urban worksite recognized for the courage of its choices and the open dialogue among the arts.

Every city is reborn many times, and as you walk through Tirana you can see some of the many fragments that have composed it. Here we are in a new Renaissance of the city. But to manage it properly, it is absolutely essential to have a vision. In the Nineties, I lived in Barcelona. At that time the city understood that one of its top priorities was to encourage and build powerful, collective works of architecture of exceptional quality. What the city needed most was to change its image and the course of events. That policy resulted in buildings that we now recognize as contemporary monuments of the collectivity.

I have the impression that you, first as Mayor and now as Minister, understood how important architecture was to enable your city to achieve its rebirth.

At the beginning of my term as Mayor of Tirana, in 2000, I found a deplorable situation: a city where, for example, there were only seventy-eight working street-lights. We were in the early stages of democracy, and the city had experienced an exodus of much of the population from the old center of the city – toward Italy and other European countries – which was more than offset by the arrival of newcomers from the suburbs and other towns in the country.

People were crowding into Tirana, living in tents set up wherever there was a public space, and tapping illegally into an electric grid that was absolutely insufficient for an urban population which had increased so drastically in such a short time. Those were times of a profound energy crisis in which I remember the utter darkness that fell over the city at night.

Your recollection about Barcelona is interesting, because it was just from that example that I learned a model of development which, however, at that time, would have been difficult to implement in Albania.

We lacked the means to "build architecture" so we decided, instead, to opt for smaller operations here and there in the city, a sort of "acupuncture": identifying sensitive points of the city and creating situations of environmental and spatial quality, introducing colorful façades, projects of urban decor capable of triggering positive overall energy that, hopefully, would contaminate the city, bit by bit, beyond the perimeters of the individual works.

Now we have reached a historical time in which this country can call itself an active workshop of contemporary architecture in the truest

TIRANA: FUTURE PROSPECTS

possible sense of the word: we can count on about seventy international architects, including eight Pritzker Price, who are working right now here in Albania.

It is a community of talented professionals of immense artistic and intellectual value, who are committed to our adventure.

We are trying, in this way, to enact a renewal that considers architecture not only as objects but as a creative force capable of generating an energy that goes beyond the work itself. The new stadium is the symbol of an incredible event in this change, and a focal point of this positive energy network.

This work of architecture was built on a platform that had already been designed by another great architect, Gherardo Bosio, who gave it the wonderful façade that Marco had the talent and wisdom to preserve, recovering it from the ruins of the building that had been severely degraded over the years. He was able to create an inimitable, multifaceted structure.

One of the nicest comments I heard about that project was came from José Mourinho who told me "Someday, I'd like to play in this stadium". That day finally came, when as coach of AS Roma, he won the Conference League cup final, and he told me the stadium was one of the most beautiful he had ever seen.

LM It really is unusual: on the inside it has a character that we could almost call domestic, with a roof that resembles a fabric, like a tent. From the outside it appears rather cryptic; it is hard to see that it is a stadium because it looks more like a landmark, with its tower.

ER That was our goal: not to build merely a stadium but create a new center of the city, for the city. We wanted to build a place where it was possible to live 24 hours a day, seven days a week. There were endless controversies and discussions regarding the placement of the tower within the body of the stadium, but now everybody agrees that this structure gives the heart of the city of Tirana dynamism, power and attraction.

Another aspect of the stadium is its theatrical character: the conditions of the site made it necessary for three sections of the seating to frame the playing field, like the stalls around a stage, and it effectively gives people the sensation of being in a theater.

Marco Casamonti worked on this aspect with the sound experts who produced an incredible acoustic system of perceptible quality. The stadium has a capacity of 22,000 spectators but the design of the space is such that their cheers are amplified to the power of sound produced by a crowd of no fewer than 50,000 people!

There is also another aspect that makes the sound quality of this stadium highly recognizable, an echo that encompasses the entire city, even outside the stadium.

At the outset, there was a long discussion on the location of such a large sports facility, but in the end we decided that it was a gift to have the inherited the old stadium set right in the heart of the city. Very few places in the world can boast such a perfect location.

LM That's a very interesting aspect, because the structure attempts to amalgamate the history of the city and its most noble fragments in a contemporary way. We know now that a stadium can no longer be considered a single-use facility, but must necessarily be versatile, at the disposal of different communities, who must be able to use it at different times of day for multiple activities not only connected with sports.

ER A central element of this stadium is the fact that it was built in the 21st century but seems, at the same time, to have always been here.

This is thanks not only to Marco's genial touch, which preserved and included the old bleachers from the earlier stadium in the belly of the new one, but also to the character of this architecture not to seem, from the outside, to be a stadium at all.

The colors make one think of a place where something special goes on, but at the same time the colored façade manages to blend perfectly with the historical complex of Piazza Italia, which represents the memory of the city, its vicinity to Italy and the events which then led to its occupation.

LM I think that giving a domestic dimension to a great collective structure is extremely important, because it means recognizing that this place is the home of a community.

ER There was a lot of discussion about the size of the stadium. Many would have liked it to be larger, with the risk of not being able to fill it with spectators. In the end, I think, it was better to opt for this more moderate size with the certainty of filling it to capacity for every match, while being able to create an intimate, domestic atmosphere almost watching the neighborhood kids play a match in someone's back yard.

LM We are no longer in a historic time of "great machines" and the beauty of this building is that it maintains the scale of its surroundings: it is a landmark but without a violent or muscular aspect, and I think this is a very important feature for a city that is changing so fast.

A few years ago I curated a few exhibitions at Palazzo Ducale in Urbino, and was lucky enough to be able to enjoy Piero della Francesca's "Città ideale" at length. I very much admire his work, and his "Città ideale" has a diversity that unifies it; this diversity also has a sense of resistance to the wear of the ages: it is a gentle, beautiful architectural design that never ages.

I have the impression that in Tirana you are working to build works that mark a new age, and that will not age quickly, indicating a future perspective. Architecture needs to live in the light; it does not thrive in darkness. What is the nature of this perspective here in Tirana, and extending to all of Albania?

FSHF
FSHF
Kjo godinë madhështore
në zemër të Tiranës
nuk është thjesht një stadium,
është shumë më tepër.
Është një simbol, është histori,
është emocion, është ...
Kjo godinë është një tempull,
tempulli i futbollit,
tempulli i të gjithë Shqiptarëve.
This magnificent building situated
in the heart of Tirana
is not simply a stadium,
it is much more than that.
It's a symbol,
it's history, it's emotion, it's.......
This building is a temple,
a football temple,
the temple of all Albanians.

AIR ALBANIA STADIUM

IDAJET ISMAILAJ

IDAJET ISMAILAJ

September 16th 2024 | I meet Idajet Ismailaj [**II**], the AlbStar Owner nd the entrepreneur who won the competition to build the new stadium of Tirana and who has involved the Archea studio in this adventure. We are seated along the fire-engine red bleachers of the new Albanian soccer stadium in the shade of the wide roofing provided to shelter the public, gazing across at the tower that is part of the new architectural complex. The interview covers topics like the need to build new monuments to bring attention to the city, and the symbols by which the community can identify itself, as well as the need to preserve the valuable traces of Tirana's architectural history.

LM This stadium has a very interesting history, because it was originally built as an Olympic Stadium, designed by Gherardo Bosio back in the Twenties. In this new transformation it is now the Albanian National Stadium. To start, I'd like you to tell me what was here before this recent work.

II The old Olympic stadium was built during the Communist era, using materials of inferior quality. The only part that was considered worth keeping was the grandstand, which was renovated and expanded in Archea's project.

After the previous political period ended in our country, we found ourselves with a large object of low esthetic value, located in a position that, over the years, had found itself right at the center of the city.

For that reason, a project to rebuild the stadium became one of the main priorities of the Football Federation and of the Government. After a long period of consultation and discussion about whether or not it would be necessary to design a new stadium from scratch, the Federation decided for the plan of reconstruction, inviting the collaboration of public and private investors.

LM So you were involved in this project as an investor...

II That's right, and from my viewpoint, it was essential to understand very fully just what the Federation needed, so that we could them adapt the their needs to the demands of the Government, which imposed precise rules in terms of public safety in view of the structure's location.

LM The location of the stadium is certainly interesting, as it is right on the fringes of the downtown district and near a number of important municipal institutional buildings and a public park.

II At this point we can say it is centrally located, that's true. When the previous stadium was still in use, this zone was largely abandoned and desolate; it was a zone that the Government and the Federation wanted to redevelop as quickly as possible.

LM So the rebuilding of the stadium was seized upon as an opportunity to regenerate an entire unresolved portion of the city and make it an incredibly lively area with hotels and services, as it is now.

II That was our goal, and we had a clear idea of what we wanted to achieve. We wanted to bring this area back to life through the construction of a stadium that would be not only functional but also esthetically pleasing, according to the desires of the Federation. We, as entrepreneurs, were able to support this idea economically in the effort to ensure the success of a project of high quality at the service of the city.

LM Let's go back to the call for tenders: you learned of this call for tenders and had to participate with an architect. How did you find Archea and why did you choose that particular studio?

II After a first approach with another architect, we got in touch with Marco Casamonti, and immediately we knew, as entrepreneurs, that we were dealing with a professional who had an immense desire to design this project and was prompted by a sincere passion.

At that time, Marco had just completed the façade of the stadium at Udine and, already before we talked to him, we knew that he would be the right person because he immediately understood what we wanted. Shortly thereafter, he sent us his first proposal…

LM … which was much more than the proposed redesign of the stadium alone…

II When Marco presented his first proposal, he warned us that it would not be the typical sort of design we'd expect for the classical idea of a stadium. In fact, its shape was very unusual: there were no right angles, and the façade resembled a sail. We knew it would be a complicated project, also from the economic standpoint, but we decided to trust him. That's how it started.

LM The proposal called for both a stadium and a tower…

II The tower would have been a landmark for the whole city: everyone would know where the stadium was. At first it was supposed to be taller, but later, due to various problems relative to the timing, we were forced to lower it a bit with respect to the original plan.

LM It think there we have an interesting dichotomy here, the way this tower participates in the project: it is a glassed structure that rests upon the stadium which, on the contrary, is a solid, opaque unit.

How would you describe the relationship with the historic structure designed by Bosio? Italian architecture in the Twenties and Thirties is an important experience for Tirana in terms of the historic and cultural legacy, as we see this also in the case of the monumental plan of Skanderbeg

Square. How were you able to maintain the historical heritage of the previous stadium?

II That was a real challenge. To maintain the Bosio façade, it was necessary to dismantle and reassemble it, with the enormous difficulty of ensuring a view as free as possible below the overhang of the new structure. That part of the façade had to become a sort of scenic backdrop and for that reason we could not place any vertical elements above it that would block the view. This meant that the entire section of the Bosio façade had to be installed beneath a bridge-like structure with an opening fifty meters wide: a tremendous feat of engineering and construction.

LM It was the length of the Bosio façade that determined the size of the newly built portion of the stadium…

II Exactly. In that portion we were obliged to put the VIP grandstand, with 1,500 seats, while on the other sides we could operate according to more classical stadium measurements. The roof was another challenge from the structural standpoint, as it is a flat roof and is not, as in other stadiums, a structure supported by trusses.

LM After being adjudicated the winners of the bid, you got to work immediately and the project was completed in a very short time frame.

II After the presentation of the final project, we needed some time to prepare the executive drawings. Archea dealt with this problem thanks to our desire to build the project in a short amount of time, which enabled us to overcome every difficulty.

LM You had a dream and built the project you wanted; but how did the public react to this new stadium?

II In general, the comments were of two types: those who from the outset encouraged us and who, still today, continue to express their enthusiasm for the outcome and those who, after a strong initial skepticism, came around. So I can say that, in the end, everybody was happy with what we built.

LM There is a widespread feeling of pride that is perceptible in the city. That the people love their stadium is very easy to understand because, in my opinion, it is one of the main symbols of the rebirth of Tirana, a monument that speaks of the beginning for Tirana of fundamental collaborations with the greatest internationally famous architects for the construction of important works.

II When public works are built with the collaboration of private investors we, as investors, have a particular feeling of pride in having contributed to the creation of significant architecture for the community.

LOCATION	Tirana, Albania [N 41°19'6.2" E 19°49'26.131"]
PROGRAM	Arena, hotels, soccer facilities, shopping center, offices, parking lots
DIMENSIONS	Area: 80,000 sqm
CHRONOLOGY	Start of works at site: June 2016 Completion of works: November 17th 2019
CLIENT	AlbStar shpk Owner Idajet Ismailaj Federata Shqiptare e Futbollit – Albanian Football Federation Chairman Armand Duka
ARCHITECTURAL PROJECT ART DIRECTION	Archea / Marco Casamonti: Laura Andreini Marco Casamonti Silvia Fabi Giovanni Polazzi
PROJECT COORDINATORS	Francesco Dall'Ò, Giovanni Cinquini, Marco Gamberi, Alessandro Riccomi, Emiliano Romanazzi
ON SITE SUPERVISION	Francesco Montani, Mattia Borrione, Sara Casciano, Alisa Bakiu
PROJECT TEAM	Susanna Fagotti, Antonio Miano, Giacomo Panfili
STRUCTURAL DESIGN	AEI Progetti
DESIGN OF INSTALLATIONS AND FIRE PREVENTION	STUDIO TI; TFE ingegneria; OE officina elettrica
SPECIALIZED DESIGN	Steps: Archest Glazed partitions: Paolo Mariottoni
RESTORATION AND CONSERVATION CONSULTANT	Istituto per l'Arte e il Restauro – Palazzo Spinelli
TOPOGRAPHIC SURVEY AND LASER SCANNER	Gaia Group
GENERAL CONSTRUCTION COMPANY	AlbStar shpk

ARENA
CENTER
MOMENTS
TO REMEMBER

The new national stadium of Albania opening took place on November 17, 2019, on the occasion of the Albania vs. France qualifying match for the European Football tournament. This is a building replacement project since it is located in the same spot were the original sports complex dedicated to athletics and football once stood, designed in the late 1930s by Florentine architect Gherardo Bosio. The building, with the exception of the monumental entrance structure of the VIP stand, was completely demolished and rebuilt with the goal of constructing a facility able to satisfy UEFA standards, to create a completely covered football complex with attached services, functions and activities able to bring the building to life every day with continuity.

Three years of construction to built an architectural work of great iconic value in place of the stadium that opened in 1946 with 15,000 seats, which became 19,000 with the enlargement in 1974 on the occasion of Albania's 30th anniversary. The demolition was necessary in order to be able to increase the stadium's capacity, to cover it any order, all the while preserving the same symbolic role that the original structure played within the city.

In continuity with the Bosio project, Archea Associati disassembled and rebuilt, philologically, the monumental façade of the VIP stand, restoring its value and role as an the element of access to the stadium's VIP areas. What's new in the concept. The new stadium features the presence of three stands, instead of four, and look like a kind of classical theater, also suggesting the idea of La Bombonera in Buenos Aires, in particular to respond to the limited space of the project area. Another distinctive element of the work is the 100-meter-high tower, where the doors of a Marriott hotel will open in a year.

In Tirana, in addition to the hotel, there are also plans for parking, commercial activities and restaurant spaces to complete the functional mix. Along the perimeter, on the urban front, there are spaces for office use, conference rooms and gyms designed to make the real estate transaction economically sustainable.

The design of Archea Associati tends to create an urban spatiality focused on the idea of increasing the value of public spaces, which create new areas and possibilities for use of the surfaces surrounding the stadium, previously denied to the community because it was an integral part of the sports facility. Building technology and envelope. The building envelope is the new sports infrastructure is distinctive in its red and black colors that recall the colors of the national flag.

All the façades, with a total surface of 30,000 square meters, are surrounding by more than 3,200 columns/brise-soleil: vertical elements, one-story high, made ad hoc and decorated in bas-relief with a pattern that recalls the fabric of traditional Albanian rugs and clothes.

AIR ALBANIA STADIUM

AIR ALBANIA
STADIUM

AIR ALBANIA
STADIUM
MOMENTS
TO REMEMBER

AIR AL
STADIU

"The tower would have been a landmark for the whole city: everyone would know where the stadium was." — Idajet Ismailaj

AIR ALBANIA STADIUM

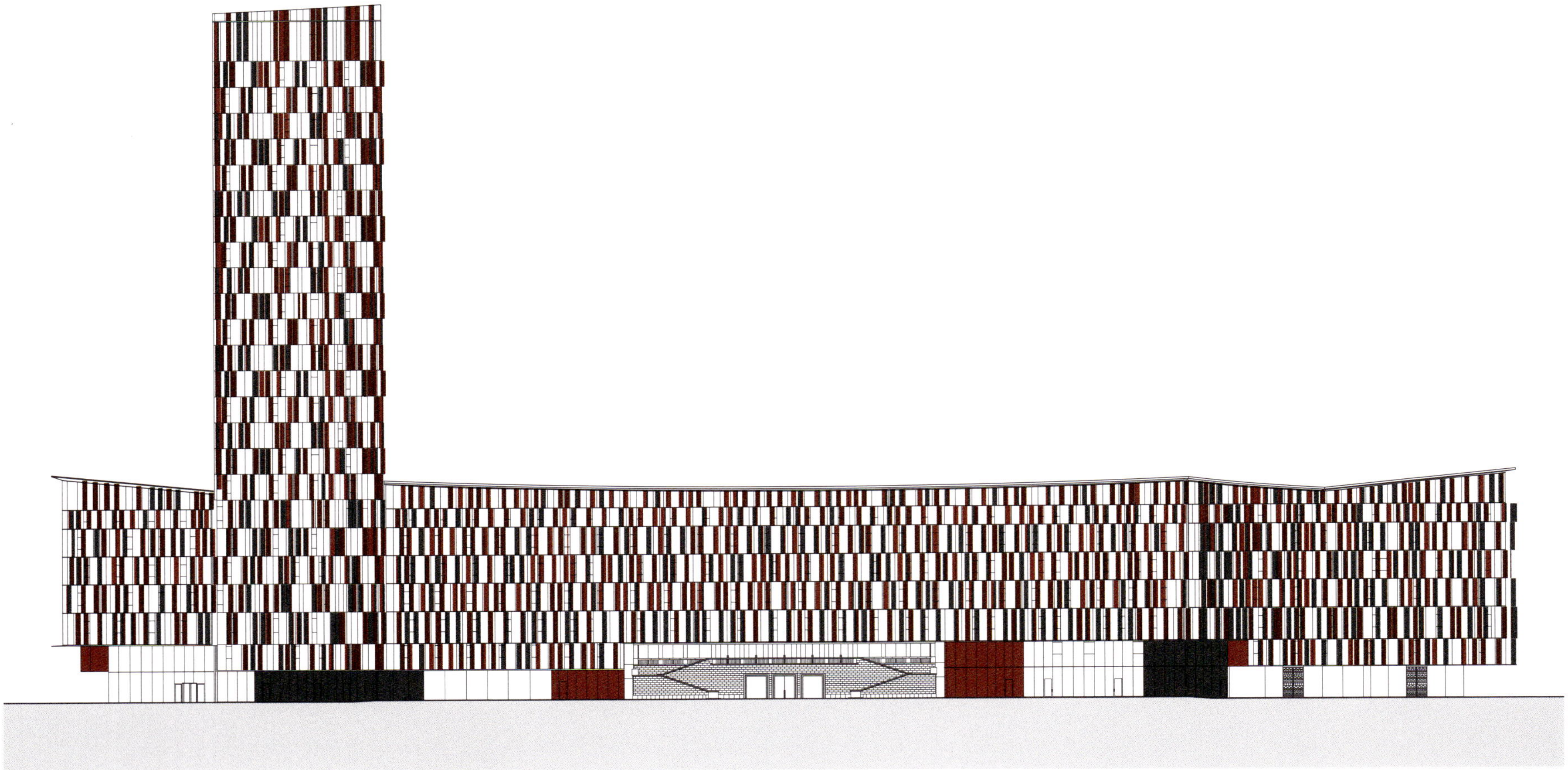

West elevation

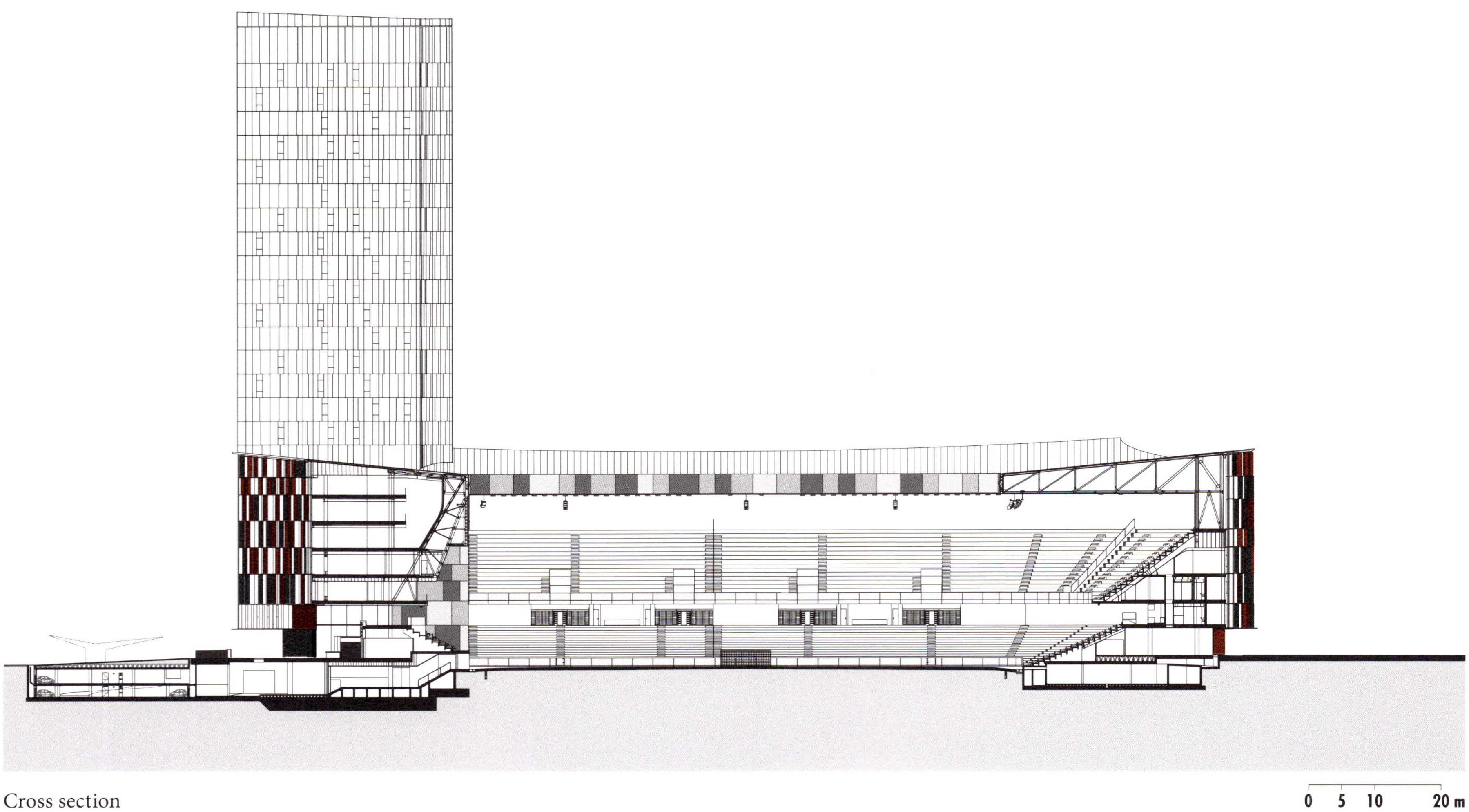

Cross section

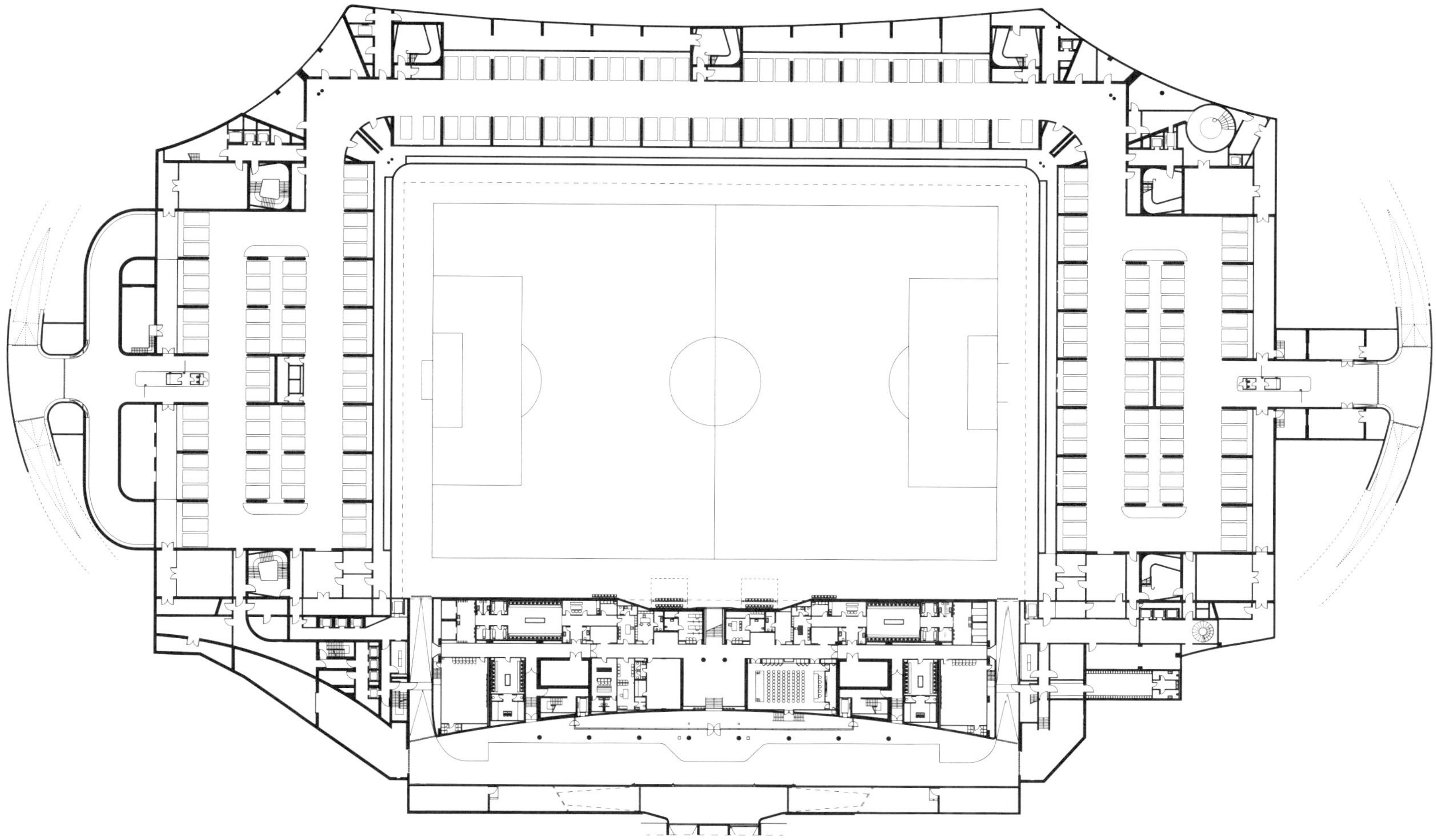

Plan L-1

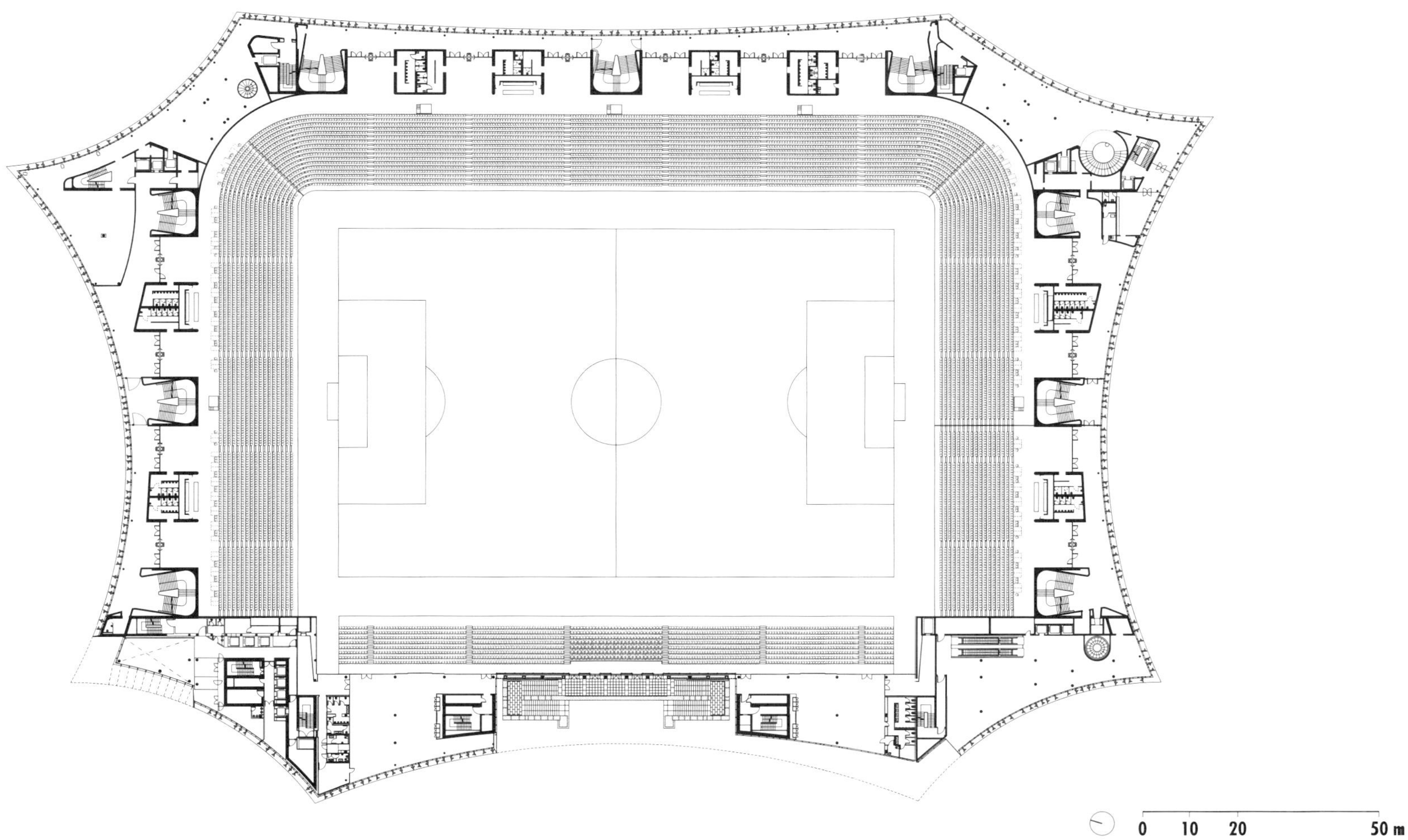

Plan L1

AIR ALBANIA STADIUM

02.29.2016 Adjudication of the integrated contract for "Design, demolition, financing and construction of the new National Stadium complex". Archea Associati studio participates as project designer for the construction company AlbStar shpk.

06.09.2016 Start of demolition of the aged Qemal Stafa Stadium, including the stratified super-structures built in 1939 according to the project of the Florentine architect Gherardo Bosio. The monumental stairway of the VIP grandstand is catalogued, stone by stone – and dismantled, to be reassembled later in the final stages of a worksite in a piece-by-piece reconstruction.

09.2016 First pouring of oversite concrete marking the beginning of construction of the base mat in reinforced concrete. About 25,000 cubic meters of concrete would be needed for the foundations, and about 18,000 cubic meters for the structures above ground.

06.2017 Start of construction on the above-ground structures in metal framework for about 6,500 tons, with simultaneous development of the corner high-rise tower with 25 floors, for a total height of 112 meters, making it the tallest building in Albania until 2022.

08.2017 Installation of prefabricated grandstand structures in precompressed concrete. The sections were divided into more than 20 types for a total of over 1,000 pieces, positioned on the lower and upper grandstands to reach a capacity of the stadium of 22,000 seats.

04.2018 Cornerstone laid for the construction of the cantilever roof, with a span of 9,28 meters and an overhang of 30 meters. Each section had to be assembled on the ground with open metal section rods, then fitted into place. The completed roof has a total area of more than 17,000 square meters.

07.2018 Start of assembly of the tower façade, which would continue until January 2019, using the same design as the stadium block for a total of 30,000 square meters. The system consists of transparent glass panels painted in red and dark gray (black), the colors of the Albania flag.

09.2018 Work proceeds for completion of the exterior. The new format of the sports facility with respect to the previous convex layout makes it possible to give the city two new urban plazas for about 12,000 square meters, in addition to Piazza (Sheshi) Italia directly in front of the monumental entrance.

04.2019 Cladding of the façade with a system of sunshade elements; more than 3,000 spindles form three-sided aluminum columns decorated with an embossed design interpreting historic Albanian woven patterns.

11.17.2019 Inauguration of the Air Albania Stadium on the occasion of the official match between Albania and France in the Qualification Rounds of the European Soccer Championship UEFA EURO 2020.

05.25.2022 The stadium is approved for UEFA category 4 and is therefore able to host international competitions: the Conference League 2021-2022 final between Roma and Feyenoord – first edition of the competition – is played there.

12.13.2023 On the occasion of a summit of the European Union – Western Balkans, the national stadium was chosen as the site of a number of institutional meetings and as the emblematic picture for the institutional photograph of all the political leaders from the member countries.

80,000 sqm	area
22,000	height
1,500	VIP seats
185	media seats
14/376 sqm	sky boxes
10	stadium entrances
54	gates
31	turnstiles
3,400 sqm	restaurant
400	restaurant tables
16	bar units
30	bathrooms
25	stair units
25	elevator centers
1,953 sqm	L0 retail spaces
5,300 sqm	totale retail spaces
17,536 sqm	hotel
80	hotel rooms
105 m	tower height
3,700 sqm	offices
247 seats	underground parking
630 sqm	bus parking

ALBAN TOWER

ALBAN XHAFERI

ALBAN XHAFERI

September 16th 2024 | We meet Alban Xhaferi [**AX**] — AL&GI shpk Owner — on top of the first skyscraper built in Tirana, where we sit poolside on the first building designed by Archea in Albania. The Alban Tower is the starting point of a new stage of urban redevelopment that will signal the rebirth of the Albanian capital thanks to the contributions of dozens of international architects and artists called to work on one of the most radical urban renewal projects of the continent. We discuss the difficulty of building and experimenting, the maniacal attention to detail, and the recollection of an earthquake that rattled the 104 meter high structure in reinforced concrete, and the tower as a symbol of change.

LM We meet at the highest and most stunning point in Tirana, in a building that was the first contemporary tower to be built in the city, and that symbolizes, in some ways, a new world. When we look out at the view from our terrace now, we can see a number of tall buildings going up, but this was the first; it all started from here.

The construction project for the Alban Tower was a technological and engineering experiment, among many other things. Can you tell us how it came about, the story behind the idea?

AX Today, building towers seems like a perfectly normal thing to do, while at the time, when we first started to think about it, it was nothing of the kind. It was the year in which we first announced the competition for the design of a masterplan for the central part of Tirana, which was eventually won by a French studio with a proposal that included eight towers. The international competition for construction of the towers was answered by three foreign construction companies: one Belgian, one German and one Italian. We were particularly interested in having Italian participation on the project because we have always felt close to that country's ideas and culture. Archea Associati entered the process by winning the competition for construction of this tower, and that was the beginning of our wonderful adventure, with Marco Casamonti, who is now a dear friend.

With hindsight, it might seem like an easy, immediate project, but it really took a lot of very intense communication, back and forth, a difficult search for the best resources and most appropriate choices.

LM If, which the work is all finished, a client can call his architect a friend, that is truly a satisfying outcome. It means that, even though there may have been arguments and difficult times, the architectural project succeeded in cementing the relationship, turning collaboration into real friendship. You are happy with the final result…

AX Absolutely… I used to joke a lot with Marco and say: "If I don't kill you first, we'll end up being best friends!".

LM When you stand in Skanderbeg plaza, doesn't this tower, with its highly recognizable silhouette, strike you immediately as having something in common with Palazzo Vecchio in Florence and with the Velasca Tower in Milan. And yet, despite these resemblances, it belongs very distinctly to Tirana; it is the city's landmark and expresses its particular energy.

When Marco showed you his first sketches, his first ideas, what did you think?

AX I think the value of an architect, what makes him different from the others, is his ability to imagine the architecture in its full size. Not everybody has that gift.

To tell the truth, at the outset, I was rather skeptical with regard to the concept of the tower. But I wanted to place my trust in the architects because their proposal expressed a particular "taste" that was very different from the architectural language to which the city was accustomed. Like everything that is unfamiliar, we have to take time, get used to it, understand it...

LM In the end, you were able to fulfill your dream of getting a truly unique tower...

AX That's right, and we are delighted. I started to understand its shape when the scaffolding was removed at the fifth floor, because that is the point at which the towers open out. I was delighted, and called Marco at once to say "You've done a fantastic job!".

It was only then that I began to understand how it would have been to imagine the tower as a whole and I think that even Marco had a clearer vision after that, which enabled him to improve even more, where possible, the success of his project. Marco is one of those architects who always want to perfect their work even while it is still under construction.

We kept running up against snags along the way, because it was necessary to find the best possible solutions through compromise between us and the architects. On this last point, Marco has always been very honest, warning us whenever our choices might have been wrong for the success of the project.

It's important to exchange ideas constantly and find a meeting point between the parties so that the investor is happy with the outcome of the work. The architect doesn't belong only to the architectural side, but is someone shared among different parties. In general, we talk more about the architects and less about the person who develops and invests in this type of project.

LM That is why we felt it important for you to give us your viewpoint... Getting back to the project, it is interesting to note that the building occupies so little space on the ground and then rises to reveal a composition consisting of four towers.

AX This aspect of the project is what I sincerely find to be its genius. Marco found this solution to make the best use of the land available and developed it upward to arrive at this iconic shape that is so beautiful to see from the outside, just in the way it opens upward: it is a true work of art. That is what the architect's work is all about: making the building a work of art by considering every detail. Marco followed the construction worksite from the beginning to the end and, even now, inquires from time to time about the health of the building.

LM Among the main challenges, the engineering must have been the most important. This is a building in reinforced concrete with a double structure in the portion below ground and in its elevation. It is an extremely innovative building for Tirana, and required an effort from the technological standpoint as well as from that of the construction methods, to make the tower elastic and resistant to the stresses generated by earthquakes.

AX The innovative aspect is very important, because when you have the opportunity to work with an architect like Marco and an engineering studio like that of Stefano Valentini, the work is balanced. The engineers did an exceptional job: the tower had a section below the ground that reaches a depth of 27 meters, and a height of 32 meters with the foundation piers. Between 9 and 17 meters of depth, the structure intercepts the flow of an underground stream. Work of the highest quality from the engineering standpoint had to be done, down to the smallest details, and this can be seen clearly visiting the basement floors of the garage, where all the structural elements are shaped and contoured to offer the maximum driving comfort.

LM Attention to every detail is the hallmark of Archea, and is visible in every single part of the tower. This enables us to predict that the building will be able to age well, even with limited maintenance. The ability to weather the test of time is a function of the quality of the details, that is then transferred to those who inhabit the tower.

The lower part of the building has a particular finish consisting of very sophisticated glass bubbles. This too is another interesting invention.

AX When the overall quality of a project is so high, all the people who work on it are inspired to give it their best effort.

To produce the cladding panels that you just mentioned, more than 200 prototypes were necessary, and the most extraordinary thing was that the manufacturer never even considered cancelling the order.

We were indeed lucky to fund so many companies that were moved by real enthusiasm to put their best work into this project. The same is true for the aluminum cladding panels: 14 color schemes were chosen by Marco and produced ad hoc for this structure. At first we had problems with certain suppliers because a few of the colors were only used for an area of a few square meters. This could be an anti-economical factor for the makers. But as soon as they saw the project, every single one of them, said no more about it. The tower is the product of a collective labor where everybody involved gave it all their best energy to ensure the success of a project that belonged to them all.

LM The color, is certainly one of the two elements, with the shape, that make the tower so recognizable. When we talk about the Velasca Tower in Milan, we think of its rosy color that is so magical on foggy days when it blends with the atmosphere. Here, instead, we have a city surrounded by forests with the mountains in the background. The tower plays with its colors in this urban landscape, and each of the four towers has its own personality.

AX They seem almost to move… the more time passes the more we are able to read meanings that didn't seem to be there before…

LM The city can see the tower from different angles and it's always different; it is a sort of "love affair" between the city and the tower.

AX Having had the opportunity to build a modern tower like this, near the heart of the city, was a huge responsibility. We didn't want to do anything that would ruin the image of the historic old city. With that in mind, we wanted to build something of great quality and we worked with Marco and the rest of the Archea team from the beginning to the end to achieve and guarantee that result. Now the tower appears as part of the city skyline in all the photographs that you see of the city of Tirana, and we are immensely proud of this because in some way it has become the symbol of recognizability of the city. In the weather forecasts on Euronews International the picture of the tower symbolizes the city of Tirana: this is unquestionably worth thinking about.

LM It means it has become an effective landmark… Also because the tower only opened a year ago, so practically it is a brand new. One last question about the rooftop, where there is an amazing pool overlooking the whole city. What does this part of the tower represent?

AX The building is organized in two sections: up to the twenty-first floor there are offices, while above it there are more flexible and "creative" spaces". The rooftop with the pool also includes a spa, a gym and a floor devoted to wellbeing. These services are not just available to the people who work in the tower, but are open to the entire city. This is a functional program, which completes the organization of a contemporary building that was lacking in Tirana until now.

LM This is what makes a building a landmark: not only its physical aspect but its vision for the future. The Alban Tower expresses a new vision for a city that is changing very rapidly.

SITE	Tirana, Albania [N 41°19'35.28" E 19°48'58.777"]
PROGRAM	Multipurpose building
DIMENSIONS	Gross building area: 21,501 sqm
CHRONOLOGY	2005-2023
CLIENT	AL&GI / Alban Xhaferi
ARCHITECTURAL PROJECT AND ART DIRECTION	Archea / Marco Casamonti: Laura Andreini Marco Casamonti Silvia Fabi Giovanni Polazzi
PROJECT COORDINATOR	Alessandro Riccomi
ARCHITECTURAL PROJECT TEAM	Gabriele Marinari, Antonio Miano
STRUCTURAL DESIGN	AEI Progetti
DESIGN OF INSTALLATIONS	Studio TI; TFE ingegneria
GENERAL CONSTRUCTION COMPANY	AL&GI

The city of Tirana has been the object of a general urban renewal plan for a number of years. After years of building chaos, where speculation produced new urban sectors that grew without criteria and without adequate infrastructure, in 2003 Tirana's authorities launched a competition to select urban growth and indicate the guidelines for the city's future modernization.
The competition for this tower, located in the city center, came out of an earlier design by the French Architecture Studio, winner of an international competition put on by the municipality. The proposal in the master plan involved building ten 85-meter high private towers, and ten competitions by invitation were put on to design them.
The tower proposed by Archea includes six floors of underground parking, 20 floors dedicated to offices, and in the highest parts of the tower, two floors are dedicated to a restaurant, a spa with swimming pool and a heliport are located at the top.
The project fits into the context, taking on the lines of the surrounding city for the principle direction of its composition; the division of the project into four parts reflects the 1920s urban design by Armando Brasini based on the city's foundation on the cardus and decumanus.
The tower takes a minimal amount of public space on the ground through a well-considered narrowing of the structure at the base, and symmetrically, a clear widening of the peak section, giving the total a marked sculptural effect. More than a contemporary skyscraper, characterised by its crystal and steel architecture, the building is inspired by the more deeply rooted tradition of the towers that animated the historical landscape. The movement of the tower's forms recalls that of the historic Italian landscape, merging them with deeply-rooted local traditions in the design of the façade surfaces.

ALBAN TOWER

"We were particularly interested in having Italian participation on the project because we have always felt close to that country's ideas and culture." — Alban Xhaferi

ALBAN TOWER

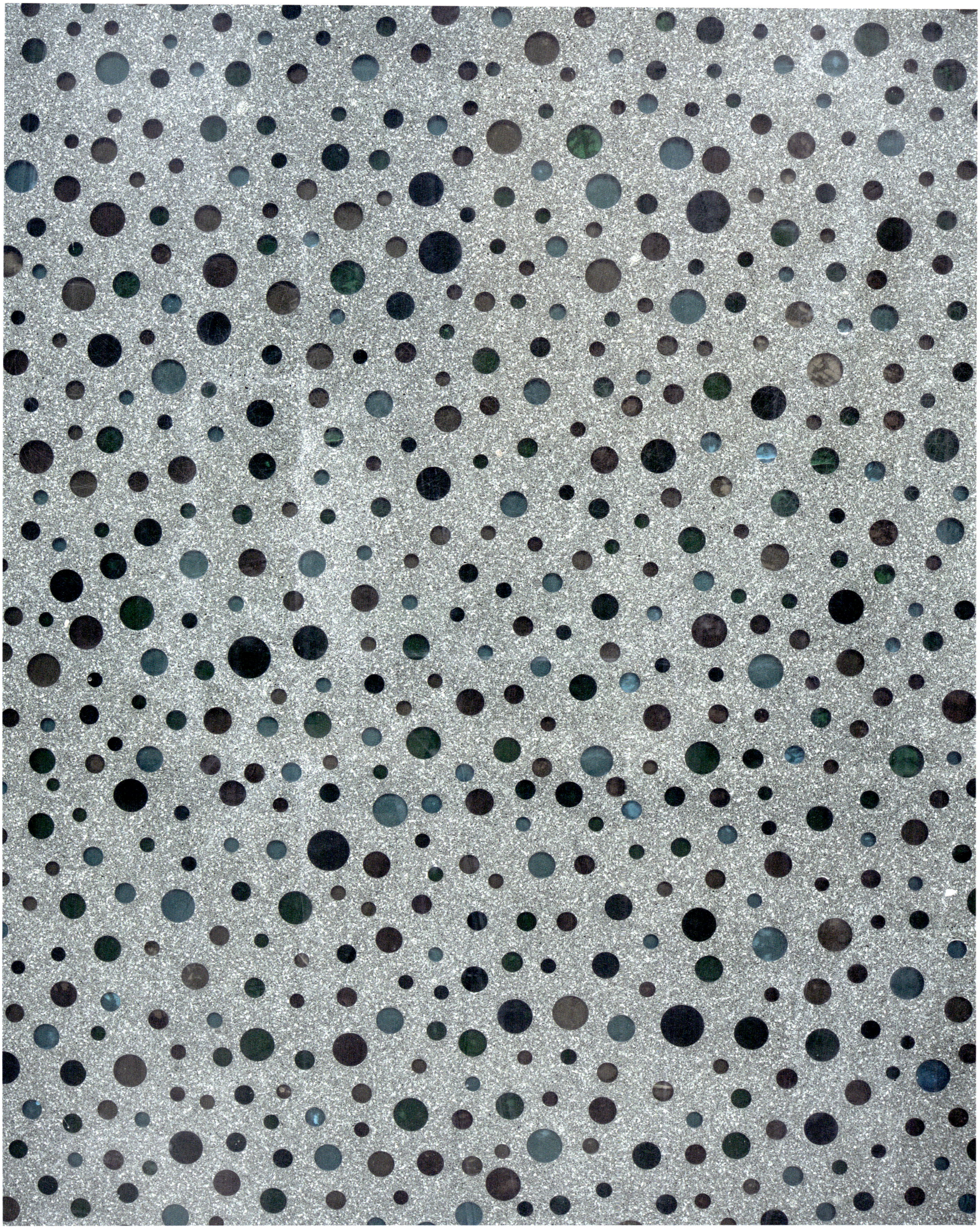

 ALBAN TOWER

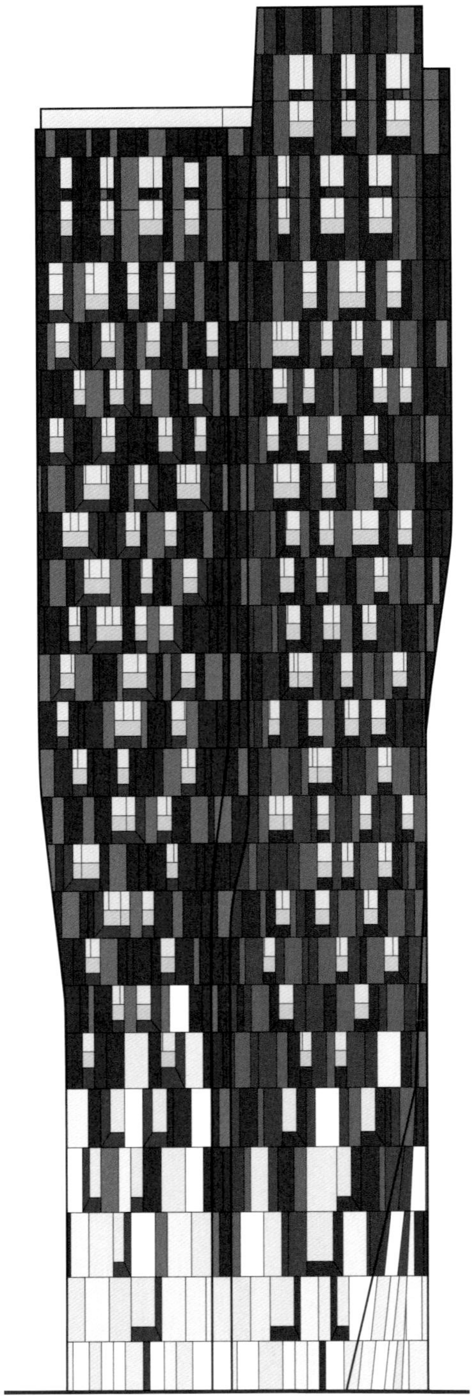

North elevation

East elevation

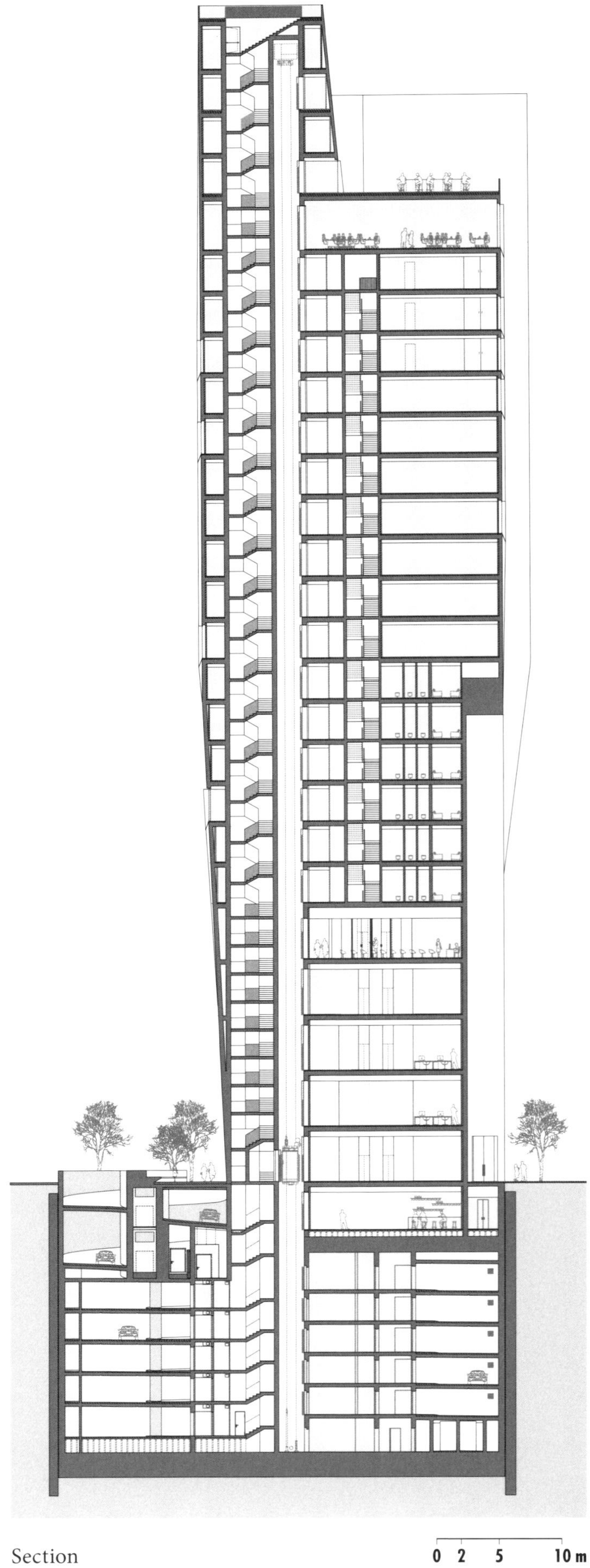

Section

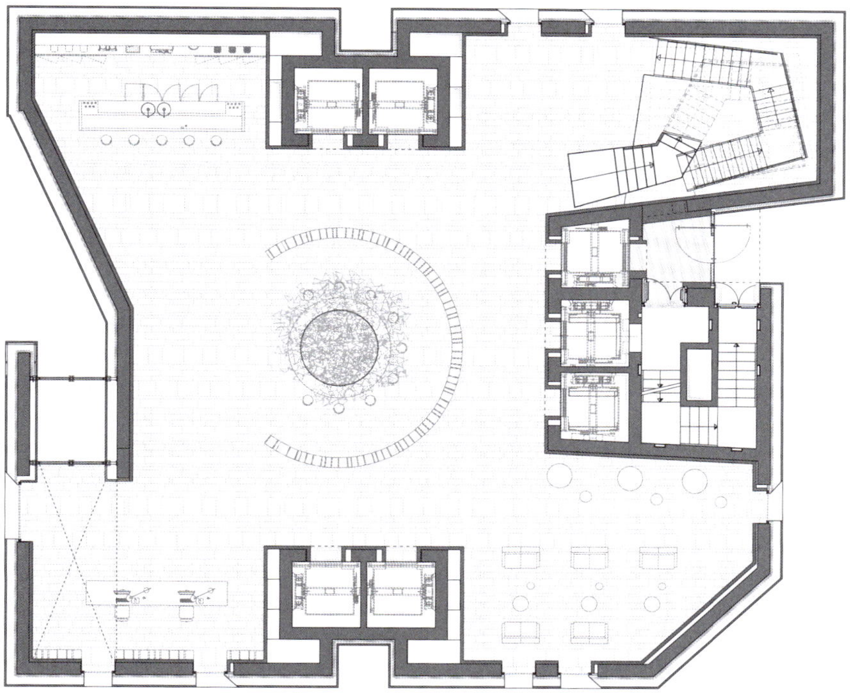

Plan L0

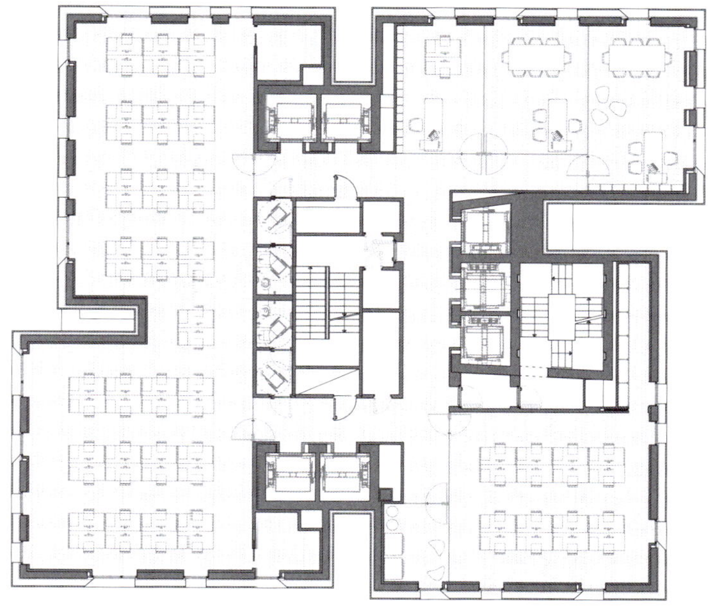

Plan L15

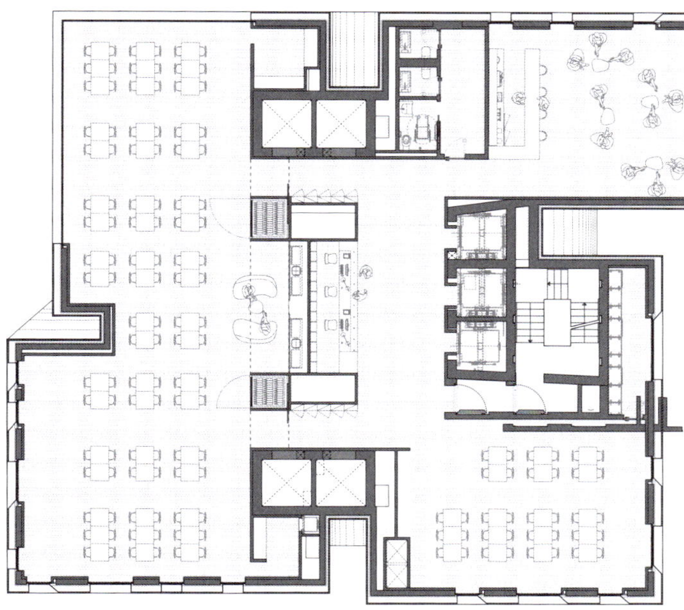

Plan L21

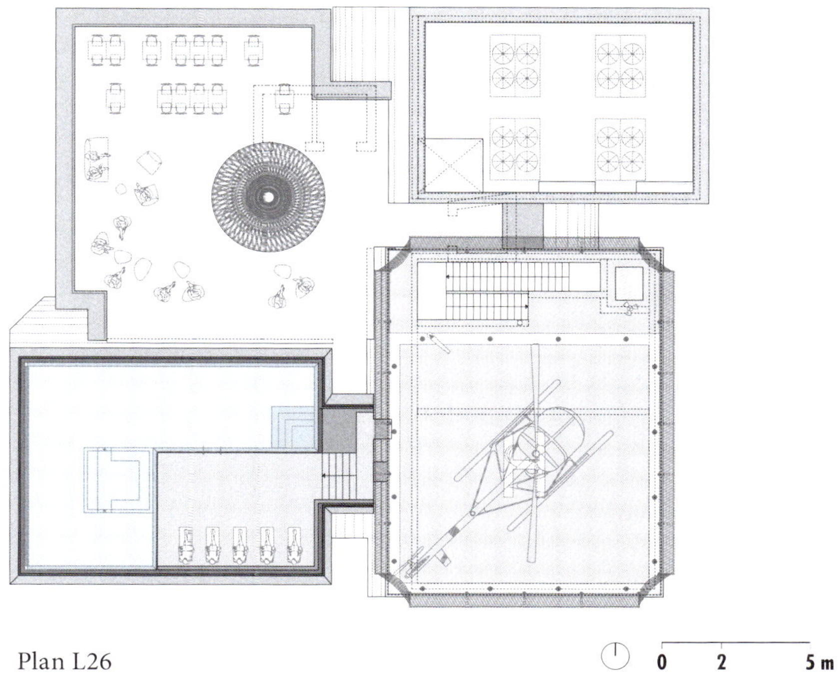

Plan L26

159 **ALBAN TOWER**

“I think the value of an architect, what makes him different from the others, is his ability to imagine the architecture in its full size. Not everybody has that gift.” — Alban Xhaferi

"It's important to exchange ideas constantly and find a meeting point between the parties so that the investor is happy with the outcome of the work. The architect doesn't belong only to the architectural side, but is someone shared among different parties." — Alban Xhaferi

11.2005 The municipal administration of Tirana announces an international competition to rationalize urban growth through the construction of ten high-rise towers in the heart of the city. Archea's project, entitled "4 ever green" wins the competition for the tower facing on Skanderbeg plaza, for the elegant plasticity of the design and successful dialogue between the identifying characteristics, blending Albanian culture and Italian architectural tradition.

02.2009 Construction of the bulkhead of secant piles in reinforced concrete.

06.2009 Start of excavation works, proceeding to a final depth of -26.50 meters, and consequent installation of five rows of metallic struts for temporary support of the excavation walls.

02.2011 Pouring of the foundation platform to a height of 220 centimeters at a depth of -6.

02.2012 Pouring of the intermediate foundation to a height of 140 centimeters at a depth of -1, to permit elevation of the tower in an eccentric position with respect to the main foundation.

02.2015 Completion of pourings of reinforced concrete, with the construction of the floor slabs.

07.2017 Start of production in the factory of the lower portion of the cladding, to consist of prefabricated panels in vibrated reinforced concrete 60 millimeters thick in four different colors, with green Alpine marble powder and granules and inserts of truncated conical elements in colored glass, with subsequent polishing.

03.2019 Start of production of the cladding in panels of composite aluminum.

03.2021 Completion of application of cladding on the façade and start of interior works.

05.2023 Completion of works and inauguration of the tower.

21,501 sqm gross building area
25 levels
107 m height

849 sqm spa
3 levels gym
rooftop pool
technical area

1,358 sqm restaurant/bar
2 levels

11,772 sqm offices
20 levels

505 sqm hall
1 level

6,504 sqm total underground area
5,420 sqm parking
2 levels
105 car park

ALBAN TOWER

BREUS
ART CENTER

SHALVA BREUS

SHALVA BREUS

May 9th 2024 | The interview took place in Florence, in the midst of the studio Archea, actually, on the sidelines of a project meeting in which the team was working on details of the project with the client after having won the bidding competition a few months previously. Unlike all the other interviews, we found ourselves discussing a work in progress, still freighted with intense desires and the problems to be overcome before those desires could become reality. Shalva Breus [**SB**] — Founder and President of the International Cultural Foundation "Breus Foundation" — is a man of great determination, who wants to get every detail just right, because he feels the responsibility of such an ambitious job in a country that is still building its cultural identity. A common home, a great roof that symbolizes the rebirth of a community.

LM I'm delighted we were able to start the first day with you. When we see the pictures of Marco Casamonti's impressive project, we see an immense covered square. It's a perfect place for greeting guests and welcoming visitors. The roof that provides shade before people enter the building is very beautiful and seems to say that this is not just a museum but much more: a house of many cultures. What is your vision for what will be the art center of Tbilisi?

SB We recognized that the museum is going to have to do a lot of work to solve an important problem: convincing the young man or woman who has just downloaded a Netflix movie and ordered a pizza and Coca-Cola to get up off the couch, take a bus or drive to the museum, buy a ticket and visit the exhibition. You can see what a huge problem it is! We figured out that the only way to solve it would be by creating a welcoming atmosphere for young people. The solutions proposed by Archea Associati work in this direction. That is why we have the lovely garden at the entrance with a protective roof over it, which comforts and soothes you with its tranquil beauty. It is all working toward this goal.

LM That's interesting, because you employ "domestic scenarios" to convey and establish a friendly relationship. The museum we visit today is not the monumental institution it used to be, with massive columns that made you feel small. It's more like a house, where people can move around freely, a home for different communities, for other times, desires and needs. It is seductive and I think that is fascinating, because culture should be seductive – it is the product of the many desires of people throughout time. What was the impression you wanted to convey with this project by Archea? What were the first elements that appealed to you?

SB My first impression was of Archea's futuristic vision. It is absolutely futuristic, because they proposed a room with a ceiling that is like a mirror, or a TV screen – over 6,000 square meters all together. It may not be strictly practical, but the effect is really stunning to have such a ceiling over the garden, over the building, it doesn't matter whether it's an old building, or a new one. It's fantastic, and this visionary idea became our starting point and inspiration. We're still working on it; it's the first thing. The second, well, in Florence, there are still Renaissance men and women even now, to my mind. The people are constantly exposed to that history and that genetic code, seeing the magnificent plazas, open to all, with the gorgeous sculptures all around, Michelangelo and so on, and magnificent architecture. They see it, live in it, walk through it every day. It can't help but become part of the genetic code of the people. I wanted to achieve the same thing, create the same atmosphere with the museum's courtyards, on the terraces, in the garden, etc., in the hope that it can bring the visitors to our museum closer to the Renaissance tradition in some way.

LM What a marvelous idea! To bring the Renaissance to Georgia, to Tbilisi, and to bring it into this museum, in this part of the world, which is, in a way, experiencing its own Renaissance.

SB A resurrection.

LM Resurrection! Life is a cycle: you die and you are reborn, die and are reborn...

SB On a different level, you are reborn, but you maintain the memory of the experiences of previous lives, previous resurrections.

LM Looking at the project, you have given it this beautiful roof – we will come back to that later – but the structure of the building is quite simple. You decided to keep the original building that formerly housed a hospital, and add an extension with space for temporary exhibitions and for your permanent collection. Can you tell us more about the nature of the foundation, the nature of the art center? Clearly, it is not a generic collection but a highly specific one with a cultural mission.

SB I'm sure you know that a museum may originate from the collection of a single donor, for example, but after that, it has to express a personality of its own, and develop its vision and long-term plans. I think that is fundamental.

So, we started with a collection of Western, Middle Eastern, Central Asian and Eastern European art. This will eventually include the Baltic countries, Russia, Ukraine. I emphasize Russia and Ukraine, because they are close to us and have exerted important influences on our culture. We'll have our other neighbors in the Caucasus: Armenia and Azerbaijan, and our West Asian neighbors like Uzbekistan, Kazakhstan, and Kyrgyzstan.

It's already a huge collection, and largely unknown to most of the world's art elite. For a very long time we haven't known what was going on in many of those places, art-wise and otherwise! The place will bring together all the artists and experts as the base of the museum, that is our dream and our vision. After the collapse of the Soviet Empire, all these new countries are struggling to break out of their national isolation and achieve recognition of their cultural identity in the modern world, and contemporary art is an ideal entry point. The world needs to discover this huge portion of the planet, with its many artists, experts and scientists and we are giving them a platform where they can be seen.

LM I love the idea that culture is a common ground and that there can be a place where different communities can develop peaceful relationships and nourish this process.

SB Absolutely. As Fyodor Dostoevsky said in *The Idiot*, "beauty will save the world." We will do our best to contribute in our small way to this beauty, which will save us all.

LM It is very fitting that this place should be in Tbilisi, which is a kind of bridge between different worlds.

SB Georgia has always been a crossroads of civilization, cultures, religions, and empires. Over the centuries we had to fight off huge empires: the Osman Empire, the Persian Empire, and the Russian Empire; yet Georgia always managed to survive. I read once that the most paradoxical rule in history is the rule of the survival of the weakest, not the strongest, but the weakest. Think of the butterfly.

I have to say that the history of Georgia confirms the rule and is an excellent example of it. This means you can survive, even if you are small and subject to the pressure of massive empires. You can survive with your culture, with your esthetics, with your religion, etc. It is a hopeful thought, at least if gives me hope. Georgia is, without a doubt, a Christian country with a strong Christian history, but it's a small balcony that hangs over a huge Muslim universe, a massive universe, and it inevitably receives influences from the Muslim culture and that of the Orthodox-Christian culture, Catholic culture, etc. It's beautiful and we welcome it and revel in it.

LM That is very interesting because, for example, we also know that Armenian and Georgian architecture was the beginning of Romanesque. First, there was a fantastic fusion of Iranian, Caucasian, Russian, and Hellenistic cultures exploring one another and blending to create something new. Then, the Armenian and Georgian monks, who traveled around the Mediterranean, eventually brought Romanesque to Italy. I think, however, that it would be more correct to say that it is not a matter of weakness over strength but of resiliency. Like bamboo: you can bend it, but it never breaks. And in this case, if you are able to maintain a strong, resilient identity, open to other cultural influences without losing your own, it will survive.

SB That's the most important thing. That's our goal for us and for all the artists who will represent the museum: to keep our cultural identity while interconnecting with the world's cultural web… that's our goal…

LM Exactly. And, coming back to the roof, you said that your ceiling is like a beautiful mirror, which is true, but in my mind, when I saw the first drawings, it made me think of the sea at sunset, a calm sea with a gentle rhythm that reflects the colors of the sunset, the weather and also the viewer's mood. Your visitors will walk beneath this peaceful image, this calm sea that joins people together: it is such a beautiful metaphor.

SB Georgia has the sea – it's on the Black Sea – and, you're right, our roof it is like the sea, never the same. The colors, the breezes and the shapes of the waves change all the time. Ideally, as you say, this roof will be similarly at different times of the day, in different weather, and when the flowers are in bloom in the garden, it will reflect their colors too.

LM I can't wait to walk under this beautiful sea!

SB You know, it's a big project for Georgia. I've had it in mind for years and this was an essential element right from the beginning.

LM One thing I particularly liked about your process was that you organized an international competition for its construction. You invited some of the top architects in the world, including Italians – which is very good! – and as it turned out, Archea won.

I wonder, what were the key points that impressed you about the project? Was it the design, the materials, the concept? How do you feel the project is evolving now that you are working together to move from the concept to the actual building?

SB We have been working very hard. What I discovered as we went along was the tremendous discipline that Archea combines with its enormous creativity, I think that is fairly rare, so it is really wonderful to find the two together. They are very quick to implement our decisions and put their fantastic creativity to work. As I mentioned, I find that they have very futuristic ideas. That is why we decided to work with them. We had worked with Herzog & de Meuron, Shigeru Ban, and other respected architects in the past, but now we work with Archea. It's been a great experience to work with them.

LM As we discussed before, and as Filarete used to say, "Good architecture has a father and a mother." He meant that it must have both a great client and a great architect, and I think that you have achieved the perfect combination for this project.

LOCATION	Tbilisi, Georgia [N 41°42'23.823" E 44°47'57.483"]
PROGRAM	Art Center
DIMENSIONS	Area: 20,570 sqm Built area: 25,000 sqm
CHRONOLOGY	2021-ongoing
CLIENT	Shalva Breus
ARCHITECTURAL PROJECT ART DIRECTION	Archea / Marco Casamonti: Laura Andreini Marco Casamonti Silvia Fabi Giovanni Polazzi
PROJECT COORDINATOR	Francesco Simonin
PROJECT TEAM	Mariia Malikova, Giulia Cerretani, Jasmine Amayou, Marianna Volpe, Anna Kolmogorova
STRUCTURAL DESIGN	AEI Progetti
DESIGN OF INSTALLATIONS	Shpetim Bucpapaj, Arjan Coka
LOCAL ARCHITECT	Archspace, Lily Abuladze

BREUS A

T CENTER

The project for the new Breus Art Center in Tbilisi was the dream of the art collector Shalva Breus. He wanted to create a cultural center open to the city and to the Georgian community. The ambitious project that grew out of that dream offers over 5,000 square meters of exhibition space, divided between a section devoted to the permanent collection and another for temporary exhibitions. However, the new building is not limited to being a mere exhibition space, but wants to be a real art center in every way, with a library, a study center for young artists, a cinema and a space for events located on the rooftop of the complex.
The choice of the site was fundamental for the development of the project. Shelva Breus opted for an abandoned property on which various buildings still stood. Many of them had been important in the past for the community of Tbilisi, like the Mikhailov Hospital.
That fine neoclassical building, dating from the end of the 19th century, used to be the main healthcare center for the city and the region. It was built around an elongated courtyard, but long neglect meant that barely half of it survived to the present day. This was the situation in which the project got its start, becoming a reflection on the concept of duality, imagining a contemporary expansion of the museum on the site formerly occupied by the hospital.
From the standpoint of materials, the new section, which would house the exhibition rooms, draws its inspiration from the existing portion, reinterpreting the pattern of brickwork but using translucent glass bricks, maintaining the same dimensions and design as that of the former hospital. This choice pays tribute to local construction methods, giving the new expansion an ephemeral, floating aspect, in a dreamlike dialogue with the past.
The distinctive element at the center of the project is the roof. It reinterprets the design of the shed used in industrial construction, becoming the unifying factor between the ancient and contemporary structures. The design of the roof is intended as a metaphor of a Georgian carpet, accompanying the visitors and showing them the way into the museum space. This element is like a guiding line that marks the different spatial sequences: the first of which is the entrance, designed as an open public plaza with a sheltering roof overhead.
Inside the neoclassical building, the roof covers a courtyard that was formerly open. This creates an original relationship with the sky and the natural light, allowing visitors to perceive the connection with the outdoors. The architectural purity and order of the existing structure are contrasted with the articulated, colorful movement of the new construction.
The color and texture of the roof play a key role in the architectural approach. The reflection of the ceramic and the shades that echo nature create inimitable effects and plays of light within the spaces. This interaction between light and color not only enhances the experience for the visitor, but is a celebration of Georgian art and culture.

BREUS ART CENTER

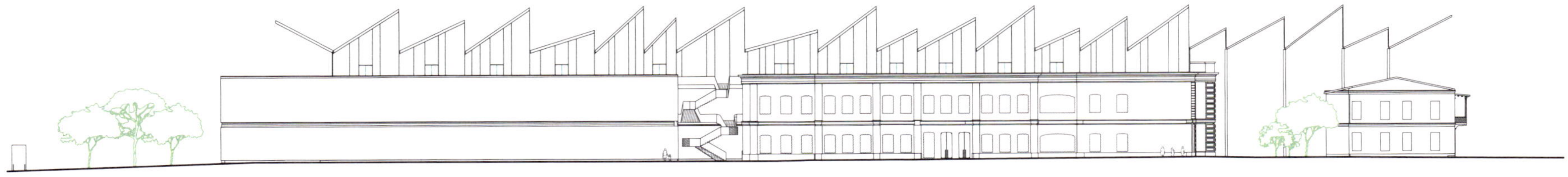

South elevation

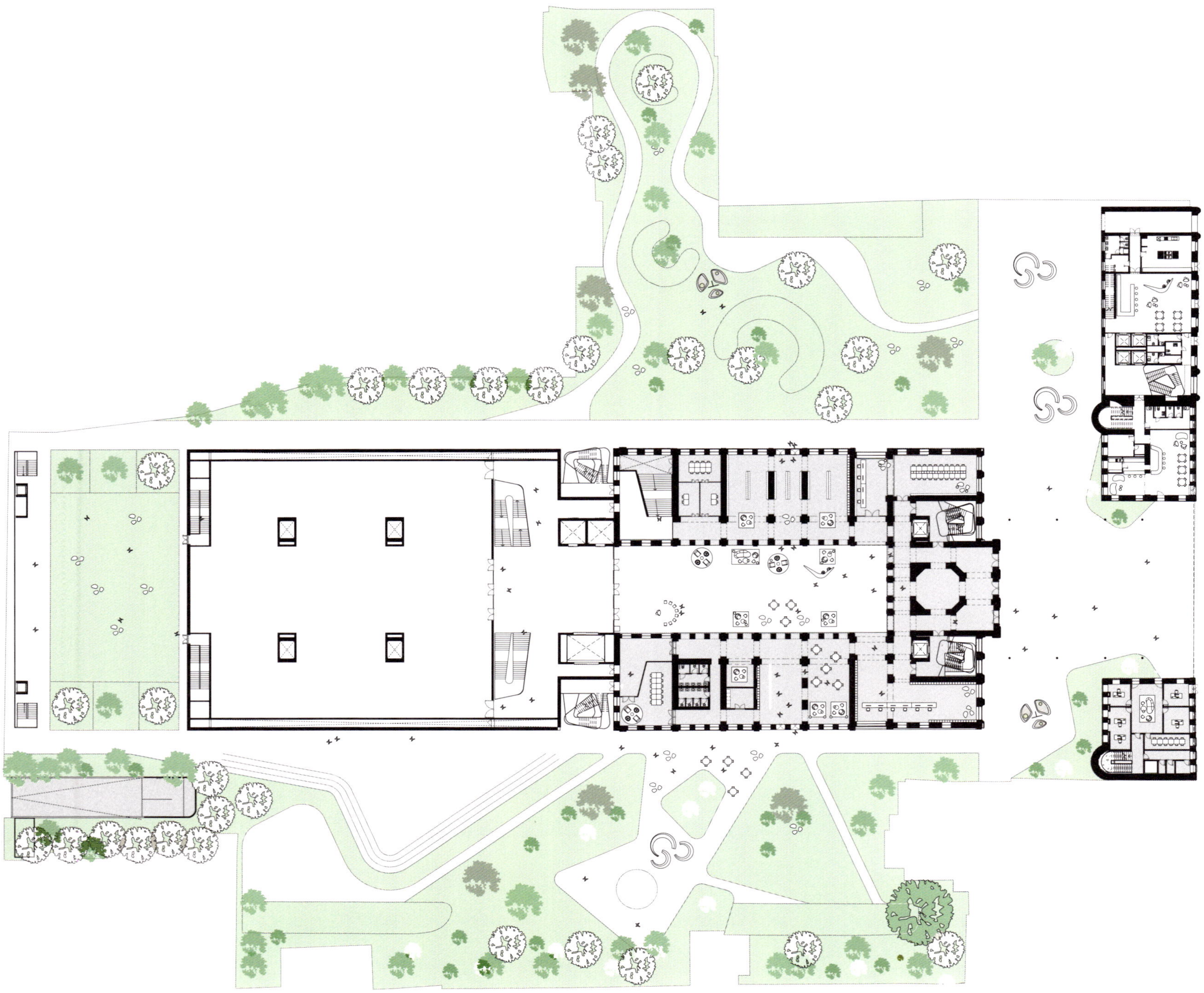

Plan L0

0 2 5 10 m

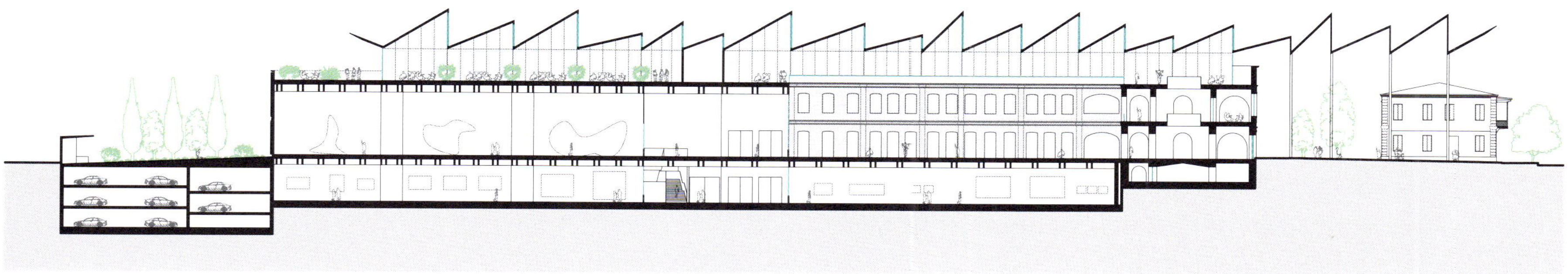

Longitudinal section

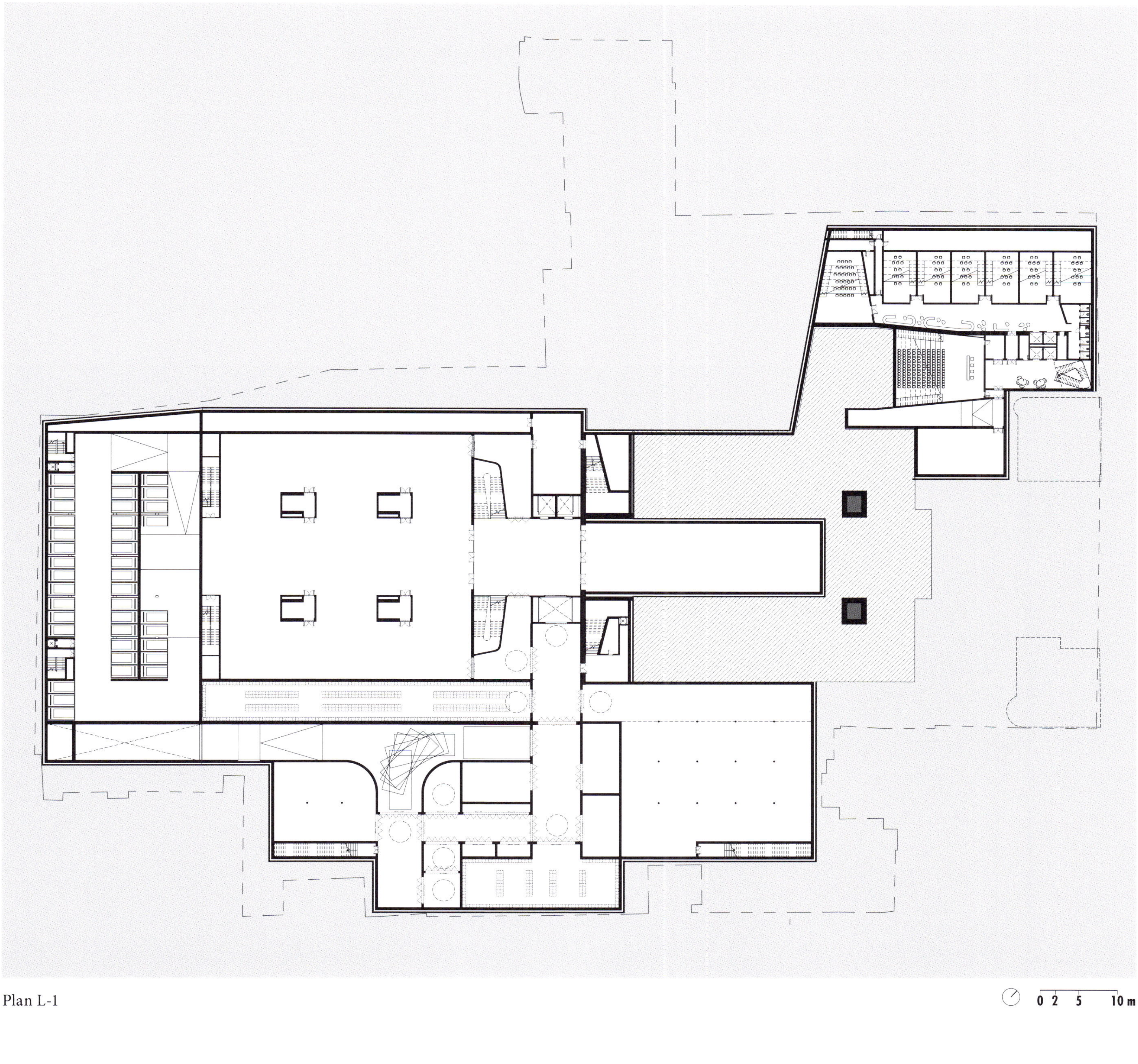

Plan L-1

06.2022 Archea Associati/MC&P are invited to participate in the competition to design the new Breus Art Center.

07.2022 Shalva Breus invites participants in the competition to visit the site. The visit is followed by a 3-day workshop/seminar and tours of the city to discover the roots of Georgian culture.

09.2022 Presentation of the preliminary project, characterized by a large roof, metaphorically uniting the existing buildings with the new expansion of the museum.

01.2024 Shalva Breus selects Archea Associati/MC&P to develop the project.

15,000 cu. m	total construction volume
19 m	height
20,570 sqm	area of lot
6,000 sqm	covered area
25,000 sqm	total area
13,000 sqm	underground area
12,000 sqm	above ground area
14,500 sqm	exterior

BREUS ART CENTER

KISS BRIDGE

DANG MINH TRUONG
HOANG VU LAN

DANG MINH TRUONG

June 6th 2024 | A line along the waterfront facing the horizon. A line that is broken in the middle by a few dozen centimeters, generating an unexpected tension. The Kiss Bridge is a puzzling infrastructure because it was built to deliver a unique experience, but at the same time it is a platform on which, every day, thousands of people gather to take the perfect picture, looking toward the ocean. We interviewed the President of the Sun Group, Dang Minh Truong [**DMT**] who worked mightily to get it built, and with Hoang Vu Lan [**HVL**] — the Design Director — who worked alongside Archea on the client's behalf, and who dreams of a Renaissance for Vietnam.

LM Good morning. We are on top of this amazing monument, a contemporary monument called "Kiss Bridge" where people can meet and talk. I'd like to hear about your vision, but first, I'm very interested in how Sun Group envisions a new concept of cohabitation in the near future.

DMT We came here around seventeen years ago when we and the other founders returned to Vietnam from our studies abroad. We are more than friends; we are a family. So it is easy to see that we start from a common ground of shared ideas and visions.

We believe Vietnam has the potential to be a very successful country for tourism, with natural resources like beaches, forests, a warm climate, and the hospitality of its people. Our dream is to put Vietnam on the map of global tourism.

For this reason, in the beginning, we focused on leisure tourism, resorts, leisure theme parks, entertainment, and whatever it would take to get Vietnam noticed, by creating beautiful destinations and iconic architecture like the Kiss Bridge. We knew that people would talk about it, would want to come and see it, and would take away experiences, memories, and stories to tell their family and friends when they got back home.

LM When you talk about iconic buildings, designing a bridge that is interrupted in the middle is certainly an amazing idea. I know it comes from a Vietnamese legend…
So, can you tell me why you asked Archea to design such an unconventional structure, and one that would be a real landmark for this place?

DMT When Marco Casamonti and I met for the first time, he invited us to visit his office in Florence and see his projects and ideas. We went to the Antinori winery, which was a type of project and architectural landmark that we had never seen before.

We discussed creating something together in Vietnam and came up with the idea of this bridge.

Initially, it was only going to be a seawall to protect the beach, but after visiting the site, Marco came up with the idea to create an "interrupted" bridge. We had never seen and never thought about this kind of bridge. So, we brainstormed, and Marco came to us saying that he was inspired by Michelangelo's frescoes of the Sistine Chapel, particularly the image of the two fingers depicted in the *Creation of Adam*. The two fingers never quite touch, but God transfers life to Adam. We took the process even farther because in every project, (especially for architecture) we wanted to have a story behind it. But how could we tell this story, which is so uniquely connected to European culture, to a Vietnamese audience?

Interestingly, the same image of the interrupted bridge appears often in our folklore. Among the others, there is one story we love to tell, about two lovers. Would you like me to tell it to you?

LM Yes, please…

DMT This is a story about a shepherd and a heavenly being. They meet and fall in love, as happens. The girl wanted to live on Earth with her lover, but because she was the daughter of a god, she had to return to heaven. The boy would have given anything to keep her with him and when her father saw how deep and sincere their love was, he allowed the shepherd to meet his beloved once a year by when she could cross the Milky Way and come to him. That bridge appears once a year on July 7th of the lunar calendar. It is a love story that the Vietnamese people know and understand.

Here, the Kiss Bridge perfectly represents this narration devoted to love stories: on the bridge's body, we can see more than four hundred phrases and poems celebrating love and love stories. On the other hand, the gap between the two structures of the bridge is filled with human sentiment, love, compassion, and so on.

We agreed with Marco in that kind of structure that never touches, where only human feelings can bridge the gap. I think this is a great idea and a great experience to tell.

LM It's a fantastic and beautiful metaphor, especially during this time of history and human life, to help people stay in touch with their emotions and with each other. Digitalization is intangible but life is a physical thing. Tell me more about people's reactions. This aspect is very important for you as an entrepreneur: how people behave and react to such an impressive landmark…

DMT If we compare this operation to our past work on the Golden Bridge in the Bà Nà Hills, we can imagine the visitors' reactions. This was a real success; even today, anyone knows about the bridge.

When we created this bridge, we were certain of exceeding the success of the Golden Bridge, because here we have a great location where the sun goes down by the sea, precisely in the gap, and this is naturally a spectacular moment, ideal for taking pictures. Compared with the Golden Bridge, it is larger and has an elegant and harmonious relationship with the sea and the sun. From here, the visitor can also look down on the clean layout of Sunset Town; that is another unforgettable view. It is unique in the daytime and even more impressive at night.

The first impression the visitor has is something like "Wow!". One of our slogans in Sun Group is "Luxury, quality and uniqueness", and everything we design encompasses these three keywords. This architecture is iconic – an icon of the culture and history of our country – and the people appreciate that very much. Thousands of people come here every day to enjoy the view.

LM So, the journey started here, with good luck and a good legend. It was the beginning of a happy, exciting adventure!

DMT Eleven years ago, when we visited this island, we were surprised by the warm climate, even in winter, and its pristine forest and landscape. Everything is lovely here.

After we went to Phuket or Bali, we thought the public at large needed to know about this place and put it on their personal bucket list of places to visit. It is a great opportunity for Vietnam to introduce a new destination and even compete with the many huge players on the global map of tourist destinations.

We now have around ten thousand rooms in this island area in our portfolio, including entertainment and event spaces also featuring live performances. We curate a show every day for ten thousand people and schedule a fireworks display every night for our guests.

This is the only island in the world with daily fireworks. When tourists give you a positive answer, you know you're doing something right!

LM This island has a powerful history because it was a place of great suffering in the past, and now it has become a place of joy and pleasure. Can you tell me more about your relationship with Marco Casamonti and the Archea team in general?

DMT Marco once worked with our partner. When we started to explore in depth the importance of design, tourism, and the role of iconic pieces of architecture, a friend of mine suggested calling Marco Casamonti because of his creativity and international/global reputation. We arranged to meet, and later Marco invited us to Florence. We understood he was the architect we were looking for. He has the great sensitivity we need in respect of values like tradition and love for innovation and the future.

LM This is a very Italian way to design…

DMT Marco is very demanding; he doesn't compromise on anything. He has very high standards and is strict in following his ideas. We loved working with him, so we are now working with Archea on another project, a vineyard in the North. And whenever he shows us his ideas and concepts, we are stunned every time. They're always unique and exactly right.

LM So, it is like a marriage between two strong personalities: the architect and the client.

HOANG VU LAN

LM We can see the bridge, standing there, and it's such an amazing "monument", such a difficult job of engineering and architecture, a "monument" that is also a part of the landscape. What can you tell me about the evolution of this project?

HVL It was a long process, actually. Initially, we thought of building a seawall in stone to protect the beach from tidal erosion. One day, our chairman pointed out that this purely functional structure could be a real livable space, a bridge, for example, that people could cross over from one side of the seawall to the other.

We began thinking of something simple: "Let's build a bridge to connect the two sides of the harbor". When we spoke with Marco, we began to see that this bridge could be more than a simple connection between two bodies of land and, as we discussed it, we began to find some echoes in local traditions. He showed us how architecture is really about tradition and innovation, and how our ideological foundations are similar. Our slogan is actually "traditionally contemporary"...

LM So, you asked Marco to combine tradition and innovation and create something unique and iconic...

HVL It took a year to finish the general layout and more than three years to design and build it... and now we are here...

LM Yes, I can understand this was very complex project in every way: also in terms of technological choices because it was being built in a very warm, tropical climate. So, what about the construction? I think this must have been very challenging...

HVL Yes, it was. Building this bridge was very complex indeed. Initially, because it was going to be in the middle of the sea, we thought the only proper choice was to build it in concrete.

But concrete is heavy, and we wanted a more graceful, slender and elegant figure. So we decided to build the bridge out of steel. This is a more technological approach, requiring absolute precision in designing every structural element of the bridge, and in manufacturing all those parts. Here in Vietnam, it was a struggle to get the right machinery and high-performance equipment to build this bridge. Luckily, we found a contractor in Ho Chi Minh City who was able to deliver the bridge on time. Over all, we employed about twenty contractors, who worked on and completed the bridge during the COVID-19 pandemic, which made things much more difficult financially and in terms of the practical operations of the construction process.

LM And then, there is a point where the two bridges meet but don't touch each other. How did you decide that a distance of 30 centimeters was right?

HVL At the time, we didn't know what the gap would be between the two sides of the bridge. We wanted it to be noticeable even from a great distance. Before construction had even started, my colleagues and I would to go out there by boat, placing the boat in the middle of the sea entrance to the harbor and looking directly at a point on the opposite side, at ground level. Gradually, keeping in mind this mark on the ground, we gradually closed the view until we arrived at the 30 centimeter gap.

We could see that 30 to 50 centimeters would be a good distance. Then we checked, and we saw that 30 centimeters seems to be a better proportion and measure for people to use: 30 centimeters is a minimum distance that allows two people to shake hands, embrace or kiss. Actually, it's the ideal distance for a kiss.

LM This idea of proportion linked to human actions and sentiments is very important because it illustrates how the entire project is in some way designed for the human body.

HVL There is also a symbolic and intensely significant meaning related to the concept of "distance". When you go to the Sistine Chapel in Rome and look at Michelangelo's *Creation of Adam*, the gap seems miraculous: the two fingers are not too far and not too close… This is very meaningful distance, a miracle: a bit wider or a bit closer and the tension generated by the two fingers doesn't work.

LM The power resides in the tension between two close objects that almost but don't quite touch… Let me ask you something more about the process of designing this bridge. What was it like to collaborate with Marco Casamonti and the Archea team?

HVL It was very collaborative. Marco is a visionary man, and our chairman is as well, so the relationship couldn't have been more exhilarating, for them and for us. They met, and things happened very fast, overnight, it was a true meeting of minds. They talked a lot about architecture, history, art, and humanity.

LM It's clear that what you have built is not just a bridge but a real work of art. It's a place where landscape, architecture, and infrastructure merge… Could you please tell me more about the beautiful curved shape you designed?

HVL Marco once told us that people need organic shapes to connect human feelings and architecture emotionally. Of course, it's difficult to build something organic, especially with a steel structure, which requires a more accurate approach to designing every part. We had to procure special software, special machinery. However, creating something organic in this sensuous tropical environment was the right choice. Curves reflect nature. This bridge represents and illustrates the nature of the place, populated by organic shapes and figures.

LM It's a way to make the bridge part of a dialogue with the geography and the landscape. We could say that you designed a new part of this geography… a sort of an artificial geography.

HVL You mention that this bridge is a landscape feature. It's true that, although people continue to look at it simply as a bridge, we see it as a feature of the landscape. Sometimes, I call it a "piazza" or "plaza." But instead of a square here, you have an infrastructure of 15,000 square meters, which on certain days, like festivals, can hold around 20,000 people.

LM I like the idea that an infrastructure, like a bridge, can be a real public space, and become an integral part of the community…

HVL Exactly. We were looking for something to promote culture and a sense of community. For example, tonight at 9 o'clock, there will be a fireworks display, and a lot of people will come out to enjoy the bridge. It really is a community space, a public space. We also organize shows on it, music events, street dances…

LM So, we can say that it is a public space more than an infrastructure…

HVL Yes, people come here to connect and enjoy experiences together…

LM I notice how you talk about the Renaissance with profound reference, Today we are talking about a New Renaissance era or perhaps a Post Renaissance. Can you connect this vision to the idea of the bridge?

HVL First, the architect, Marco, comes from Florence, and this counts. Somehow, the Renaissance is already in his blood. So, whatever he does, he always draws from his culture and history: the Renaissance. In designing a bridge like this, he was certainly influenced by the Renaissance. This Kiss Bridge celebrates people, in the most positive and delicate sense of their humanity; I have no trouble calling it "humanism", as it certainly echoes the values promoted by the Renaissance.

The mission of this bridge is to encourage human relationships: a handshake, a kiss, a hug, expressions of friendship or love. With this in mind, we named the bridge by its role, not by emphasizing the gap. We wanted to show how human touch and connection are always possible, especially during this period of history where, due to conflicts, everything seems to be disconnected and polarized. To show that we are closer than we think, if we just reach out a little.

LM Why do you think this bridge can be important for your country, which is experiencing a new phase of development?

In Vietnam, we can be proud of many things, like nature or history. But in terms of architecture, we haven't had much, so far, to be proud of. With Marco, we tried to build a work of architecture that could become a symbol or an icon: it is the perfect image to representing this island and, even more, our country. It's a symbolic image of what is happening not only here but in Vietnam generally. This is the new image of Vietnam.

LOCATION	Phú Quốc, Vietnam [N 10°1'41.312" E 104°0'14.1"]
PROGRAM	Pedestrian bridge
DIMENSIONS	Total area: 14,820 sqm Built area: 1,910 sqm
CHRONOLOGY	Design: 2019-2022 Construction: 2021-2023
CLIENT	Sun Group
ARCHITECTURAL PROJECT, AND ART DIRECTION	Archea / Marco Casamonti: Laura Andreini Marco Casamonti Silvia Fabi Giovanni Polazzi
PROJECT COORDINATOR	Luana Carastro
ARCHITECTURAL PROJECT TEAM	Camilla Alzate, Francesco Giordani, Anh Nguyen, Giacomo Pazzaglia, Alessandro Rizzi
STRUCTURAL AND INSTALLATIONS DESIGN	F&M Ingegneria
GENERAL CONSTRUCTION COMPANY	Sun Group

The Kiss Bridge is the product of a profound reflection on the concept of connection. Rather than imagine a bridge capable simple of connecting two points from A to B, the project focuses on creating an emotion by building an infrastructure that symbolizes the desire to meet, to join, to kiss.
That is the origin of the bridge named Kiss Bridge, consisting of two long, curved arms that, after rising gently slowly toward the center point for over 400 meters, reach a height at the central spans of 16 meters above sea level, where they stop, almost touching, but without joining together. The physical separation of just 30 centimeters means that people cannot to pass from one to the other of the two shores, and can only lean across to touch, shake hands or kiss.
It is this separation that holds the deepest meaning of the work, which is to join people not physically, but virtually, transferring positive tension and energy from one side to the other and evoking the image of the hands stretched toward one another in the *Creation of Adam* by Michelangelo in the Sistine Chapel.
The inspiration for the bridge derives from the Vietnamese legend Ông Ngâu Bà Ngâu which tells of the impossible love of a goddess for a mortal man. Their passion is so strong that the emperor grands them the right to meet only once a year on a magic bridge created by a flock of birds. The goddess and the mortal will love one another without ever touching, a platonic union typical of the great loves that withstand enforced distance.
The purpose of the work, entirely evocative and symbolic, offers the opportunity of creating a meeting place for people but also ideally linking two different sides, experiences and cultures.
A bridge that does not reach the opposite shore might seem superfluous, however think how amazing it must be to reach one of the two ends just to kiss the person we care about, better yet, to do it just as the sun is setting right there in the middle. I wish every person who visits this place could have such an unforgettable experience.
Kiss Bridge is built on the existing breakwater, but its structure is divided into several parts: the accesses to the bridge from north and south, a pedestrian walkway integrated with the restaurants – Mr Bridge on the north side and Mrs Bridge on the south side – a photoshoot bridge that functions as a panoramic platform toward the Kiss Point. Given the particularity of the place and its specific structural identity, the choice of the materials relies on the standards for local coastal and maritime structures, concentrating largely on the use of local materials: gray granite and painted steel. The piles and abutments of the bridge are in reinforced concrete, while the deck applies a solution using torsion-proof metallic formworks with the bed in collaborating reinforced concrete.

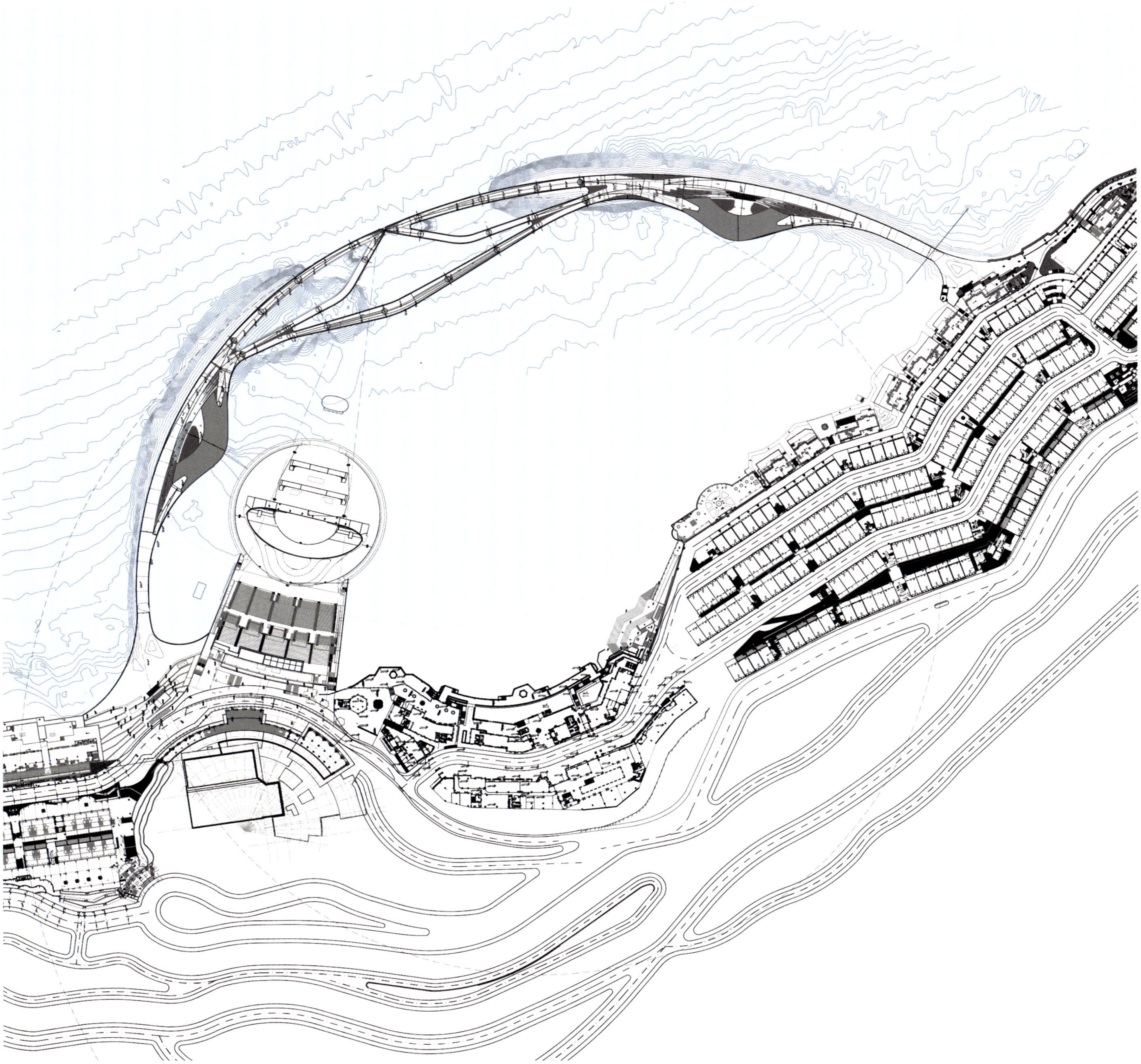

Masterplan

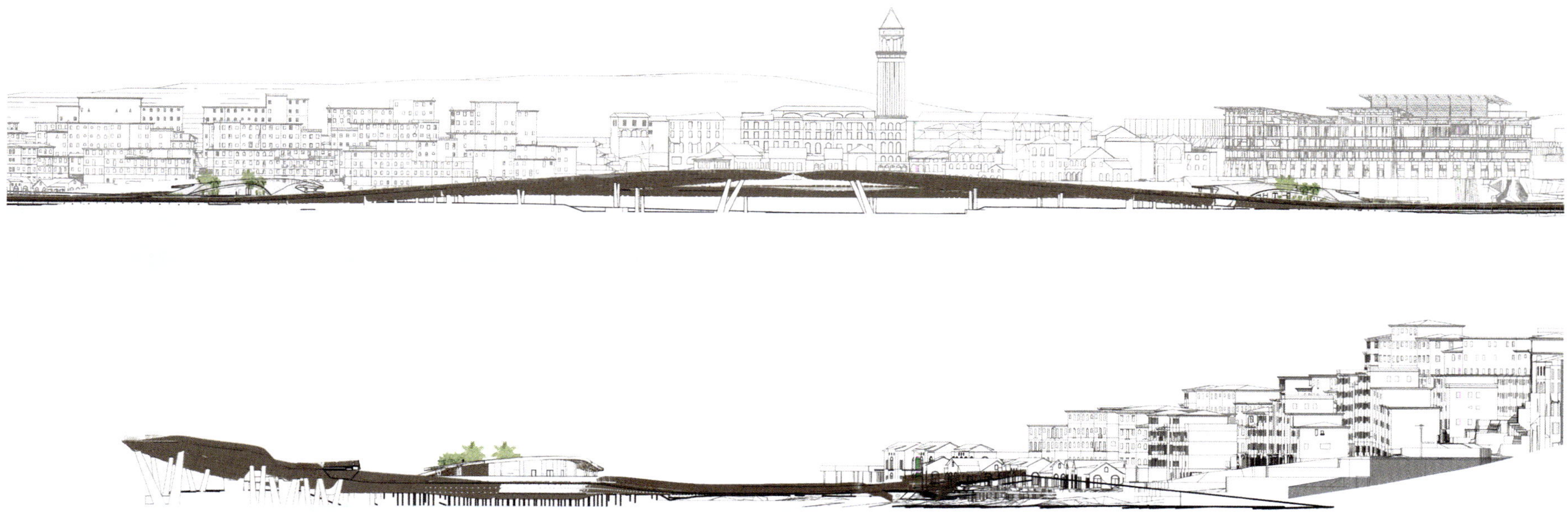

0 10 20 50 m

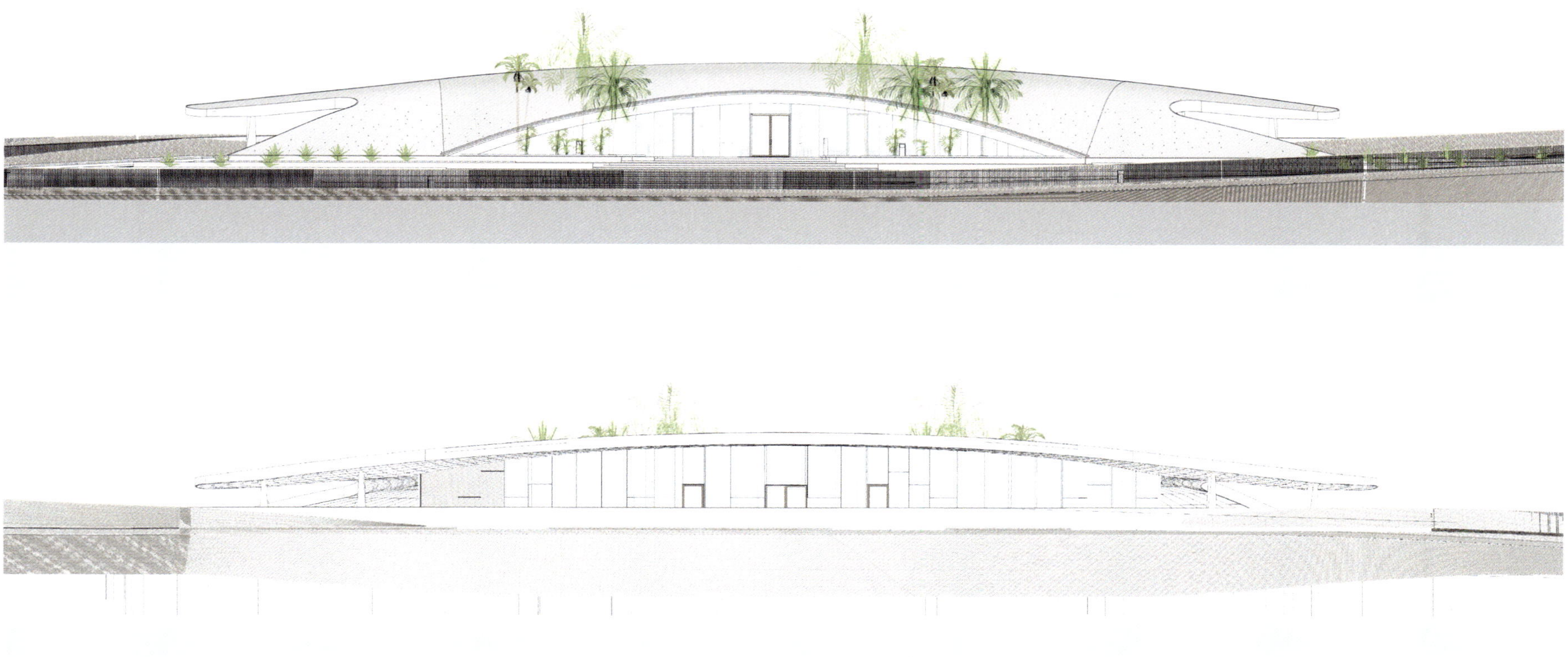

Elevations

0 2 5 10 m

KISS BRIDGE

"We wanted to show how human touch and connection are always possible, especially during this period of history where, due to conflicts, everything seems to be disconnected and polarized. To show that we are closer than we think, if we just reach out a little."

— Hoang Vu Lan

KISS BRIDGE

07.2019 Presentation to the Sun Group of the first concept of the project.
In this initial stage, Archea presented its first concept of the project to the client. This presentation included preliminary ideas and an overview for the design and functionality, intended to garner feedback and determine a clear direction.

11.2019 Design Concept approved.
After revising and discussing the project at some length, the design concept was officially approved. This passage was an important milestone, because it provided a solid basis on which to build the subsequent project development.

08.2020 Schematic Design approved.
In this stage, the project acquired a more detailed form with the presentation of the schematic design. This included more specific layout drawings and a definition of the functions of the spaces. Approval made it possible to go forward toward the construction detailed.

02.2021 Design Development – D1800 Foundation approved.
The Design Development (DD) of the foundation was approved. This stage required in-depth planning to ensure the stability and sustainability of the structure.

04.2021 Design Development approved.
At this time, the final approval of Design Development confirmed that all the project details were in line with the standards required, opening the way for the effective construction of the project.

08.15.2021 Cornerstone.
The ceremony of laying the cornerstone officially marked the start of construction. This symbolic event was the first step in actual realization of the project.

03.2022 Interior Design Concept of two restaurants approved.
The concept for inclusion of two restaurants was approved, expanding the original vision of the project and introducing new culinary experiences for the users.

04.29.2022 Visit to the steel mill in Vietnam.
A team of engineers and architects from Archea visited the QH Plus steel mill in Vietnam to verify directly the quality of the steel segments.

11.25.2022 Installation of the Kiss Point.
The installation of the Kiss Point of the bridge was the most significant event of the project for the structural and architectural components involved.
The installation of the projecting sections is a fundamental passage that contributes to the functionality and esthetics of the entire project, guaranteeing a distance of 35 centimeters between the two terminal points of the bridge, and thereby demonstrating the very concept of the Kiss Bridge and the installation of a work of performative art, which encourages public participation and recovery of the feeling of connection.

12.22.2023 Inauguration / Soft Opening.
The conclusive stage of the project led to the inauguration. This stage was fundamental to ensure that everything functioned perfectly to create a positive experience for the future visitors.

6,385 cu. m total volume of construction (calculated only on the volume of the restaurants)

6,865 cu. m total volume of construction (calculated including the ticket offices)

1,910 sqm built area

14,820 sqm total area

800 m radial length

16 m height of Kiss Point (above sea level)

1,360 m length of bridge roadways

6,800 sqm public roadway area

480 sqm area of public ticket offices

639 sqm area of public restaurants

136 sqm area of public rest rooms

396 perforated panels

238 steel segments

ECEPDI ENERGY CENTER

OFFICES

GU JIN

GU JIN

June 21st 2024 | We meet Gu Jin [**GJ**] — Former President of ECEPDI (East China Electric Power Design Institute) — on the top floor of the ECEPDI head office in Shanghai. Enclosed within its glass walls we observe the uninterrupted flow of traffic in the network of street below, but the goal of this building is to be unique and different from the forest of anonymous buildings that surround it. This floor was designed for the leisure time of the employees and guests, with large rooms interspersed with terraces. The client is very cordial and exhibits personal pride in having successfully completed a work that Shanghai now considers a landmark for its strong personality.

LM Good morning. Let's start our conversation about the new Archea designed building in Shanghai, which I consider very impressive. It seems to be to be a sort of contemporary monument for a new community, a better, more ecological community.

Let's start from the beginning. A competition was held and many architects were invited. You chose the Archea project. Can you tell me first what the competition program was for this building? What were the requirements?

GJ Yes, we used an international public bidding process. We wanted the building to be future-oriented: green, low-carbon, energy-saving, environmentally friendly, healthy, and comfortable. It also had to be designed to be open and shared by employees. Located at a critical intersection in Shanghai – where the Inner Ring Road meets the Wuning Expressway – we hope this building will become a prominent landmark and a significant destination.

Archea's proposal was fully aligned with our bidding goals in 2020. At that time, I was particularly surprised by Archea's building design. In addition to being my own preference, many other architectural experts in Shanghai unanimously selected Archea's plan.

LM Why did they choose Archea? I know there were different proposals, so what was your main reason for choosing this project over the others?

GJ A truly remarkable building must have a soul. The building, designed by Archea, blends Chinese and Western elements and creates a stunning impression. It is intended to be a landmark in the area, one that will retain its significance and prominence in the years to come. This building is meant to evoke a strong sense of monumentality, serving as a lasting and influential presence in the region.

LM I completely agree with you. I was impressed by this building when I saw it for the first time because it is so utterly different from all the other buildings in Shanghai. It has a strong personality; it is open and monumental at the same time, a monument that is not tyrannical or violent but that exhibits a gentle, yet strong vision for the future.

The Company it was built for produces electricity and energy for the country. So, sustainability is at the very least one of the most if not the most important mission: we must become more sustainable.

What is your idea of this architecture being sustainable? What is it about the building that expresses its sustainability?

GJ This is mainly reflected in the selection of materials. When selecting materials for our building, we prioritize natural and environmentally friendly options, such as fair-faced concrete, corten steel, and enamel panels. These materials are chosen for their green credentials.

Our fresh air environmental protection system also features a low-carbon, energy-saving design to enhance sustainability and reduce environmental impact.

LM So, this building is basically a master class in how to improve architectural practices in China.

GJ Yes, it is. For example, our fresh air and air conditioning system is significantly more economical than the traditional systems used in China. It saves over 33% of the energy and uses about 700 square meters less space. These efficiencies are significant in a city where every inch of space is valuable.

LM Good architecture needs good architects but also good clients. I know that you were key in pushing this project for the best results. I also know that during the project process, there were a lot of problems and more difficult of coordination than normal building, to overcome a lot of issues.

What do you think about the importance of being a good client for such good architecture?

GJ The most important thing is that Archea Team and Giovanni Polazzi produced an extremely good design for this project, combining Chinese and Western elements. This enabled us, as a client, to bring excellent domestic and foreign suppliers whole-heartedly to this construction site. We must remember that this building was built from 2020 to 2023, during a very difficult and challenging period for all concerned.

The client and the owners play a vital role, including in the choice of excellent local suppliers, in line with the low-carbon and environmentally friendly nature of our building. This includes the relationship between Archea and our domestic partners as well as the relationship with the government: our team, including myself, was deeply involved in the entire process. This was necessary because the difficulty of constructing this building was enormous.

LM The quality of materials and details is very good. I agree with you that architecture is the result of dialogue between different parties who have to work together to achieve the best result.

You have spoken of 'community' many times, and this is a building for a very large community, primarily young people working here to design the future with a unique energy.

So, this building represents an idea of community. It also provides exciting spaces to stay or work because, since the pandemic, the way we live in our offices has changed quite a lot. What is your idea of community and good architecture for the future of working space?

GJ The internal design of this building is intended to foster sharing and communication, creating an environment and atmosphere in which our employees, especially the young ones from around the world with diverse educational backgrounds, can thrive. Combining Chinese and Western elements in the building design has transformed the workspace, making it distinct from our old office building. This new environment changes the physical setting and alters how our employees, including those with foreign educational backgrounds, feel and interact. Through such a physical environment, we aim to attract excellent young people and provide them with a unique and inspiring workspace. Moreover, after this building was completed, our employees and their families and friends were eager to visit the building and come here to socialize.

LM This shows that people find it a congenial living space. We always say that the office is like a second home. It follows that if the second home is well designed, people work well and have pleasure staying there. I really like that this building has a lot of space; it's a generous building, and this makes people feel good, doesn't it?

GJ In the current Internet age, personal communication is becoming less frequent. We aim to provide an open and shared environment that fosters pleasant and effective communication among our employees, both internally and externally. This was my primary goal for the design of the environment. Secondly, the Archea design of our building was chosen because the floors cover more than 3,000 square meters, creating a vast, continuous space. If dividing this space into smaller, enclosed areas would negatively impact the employees' working environment, light, and overall experience. Another critical consideration is cost control, particularly for the ventilation and air-conditioning systems. By not having partitions and using suitable materials, we can manage costs more effectively, ensuring efficient use of our budget. This allows us to keep expenses under control while maintaining a comfortable environment.

LM After the competition, did you follow every step of the construction process? What was your relationship with the building while it was under construction? What were your feelings and concerns?

GJ The design of this building is unique, which made the construction process particularly challenging. There are plenty of memorable stories about the issues we encountered and how we solved them. One example that stands out is the construction of the spiral staircase and the fair-faced concrete exterior, which were particularly difficult to execute.

Another significant challenge was related to the fresh air conditioning system. Archea's original design called for a low-carbon fresh air system, which was quite advanced and common in Europe. However, we initially decided not to implement it due to cost considerations and a lack of familiarity with the system among our domestic designers.

Fortunately, our team and the owners were committed to maintaining the integrity of Archea's design. Through persistent research and exploration, we eventually found a suitable fresh air conditioning system designed and supplied in China. This allowed us to adjust our plans and implement a system aligned with the original low-carbon concept.

The owners, consultants, designers, and construction teams worked collaboratively and supported each other throughout this process. In the end, we successfully implemented the fresh air system as initially envisioned by Archea, enhancing the working environment for our employees and providing a more comfortable and sustainable space.

Regarding the challenges we faced, my determination, along with the efforts of our preparatory team and the expertise of our power engineering and design technology teams, played a crucial role. Our management experience also contributed significantly. The difficulty required us to make continuous adjustments throughout the process.

For instance, we used a drone to film the building and its unique features, including the spiral ramp, for publicity. One notable story involves the shock absorbers used in our power plant. These shock absorbers, typically used beneath our 3,000 steam turbine stabilizer, were ingeniously applied to our rotating ramp.

LM I'm very impressed because this building uses Chinese technology, and the quality is very high. It's a combination of Italian design and Chinese production.

I know you love art and architecture in your private interest, and this idea of this building being a sort of cloud creates a poetic and stunning image. What do you think about this poetic wing motif that makes this building unique and visionary?

GJ This element can be found in pavilions and traditional buildings in China, such as terraces and open halls. Specifically, we faced significant challenges during the construction of the ground floor and the cloud top on the 15th floor. The complexity and difficulty of these tasks were substantial.

LM The building seems to float, like a floating building.

I'm curious now about the reaction of people who visit the building now that it's complete and more and more people are walking through it. When a building features impressive architecture, it often surprises visitors. What was the initial reaction of people discovering this building? What aspects of the design were unexpected or surprising to them?

GJ People were very shocked by the building. Creating such an impressive structure took just four years from planning to completion. The reactions to specific features, such as the spiral staircase, the fair-faced concrete, and the enamel panels on the facade, were particularly notable. Additionally, many employees shared positive feedback about the internal environment, particularly praising the fresh air and air conditioning systems for providing a comfortable atmosphere. Many of our colleagues said they felt as though they worked in a modern museum…

LM That's excellent feedback! Shanghai is the city of the future. You always produce the future here, so this building represents another fragment of your future for this city and this country.

GJ The building is intended to be a significant example of contemporary architecture. Our building will hold an essential position in this context. Just as buildings in Florence are celebrated for their enduring appeal, I hope our building will also remain relevant and will continue to be admired for the next 100 or 200 years, preserving its youthful significance…

LM It is a contemporary monument for Shanghai, and I'm sure it will!

Last question for you: what is your favorite place in this building? I mean, the place you love the most…

GJ There are so many! I cannot pick just one! The building is not only a perfect work of architecture but also represents a successful collaboration with Archea. This project marks the beginning of what I hope will be many more achievements. Although Archea has been in China for over ten years, the building of the East China Electric Power Design Institute is really an important milestone. I hope we can contribute significantly to Shanghai's urban renewal and development. I aim to continue participating in these efforts, contributing whatever I can to future projects.

SITE	Shanghai, China [N 31°14'40.923" E 121°24'47.016"]
PROGRAM	Offices
DIMENSIONS	Built area: 74,460 sqm
CHRONOLOGY	2021-2024
CLIENT	East China Electric Power Design Institute
ARCHITECTURAL PROJECT AND ART DIRECTION	Archea / Marco Casamonti: Laura Andreini Marco Casamonti Silvia Fabi Giovanni Polazzi
PROJECT COORDINATOR	Carolyn Spoljaric
ON SITE SUPERVISION	Gao Ying
ARCHITECTURAL PROJECT TEAM	Wenbin Sun
STRUCTURAL DESIGN	ECADI
INSTALLATIONS AND FIRE PROTECTION DESIGN	ECADI
GENERAL CONSTRUCTION COMPANY	China Construction First Group Corporation Limited

Construction of the new Shanghai offices of the East China Electric Power Design Institute got under way in January 2021. The building, designed by Archea Associati with the support of ECADI – East China Architectural Design & Research Institute for the structural design, was built with the goal of renewing the existing urban fabric.
The project aims to integrate various functions within a single block, in which a wide range of facilities can be centralized, making the building more economical and efficient. The work had to fit in with the existing setting and adapt to the characteristics of the site, taking account of the urban landscape and requisites of general planning, as well as of the desire to make the structure a landmark of the company itself.
The property faces on two main roads in the city of Shanghai: Wuning Road to the east and Zhongshan North Road (Inner Ring Elevated) to the south, a position that gives it the potential to become a reference point in the city. The building has two entrances on Wuning Road, one used as the main entrance and the other as a secondary entrance for vehicles and pedestrians.
The characterizing element of the entire building is a long ramp (1 kilometer) in Corten, positioned on the east side of the building, with access to the various floors, while two ramps on the west and southeast sides lead to the underground garages.
The building develops on sixteen floors above ground for an area of 50,000 sqm plus two underground floors of 25,000 sqm, for a total of 75,000 square meters.
The lower floors house various functions such as a reception lobby, meeting rooms, an exhibition area, gym, conference rooms and archive. The intermediate floors are open-plan, intended as work areas, while the upper levels are divided into management offices and meeting rooms. The roof is characterized by a more recreational function, featuring a small bar and a garden.

“A truly remarkable building must have a soul. The building, designed by Archea, blends Chinese and Western elements and creates a stunning impression.”

— Gu Jin

ECEPDI ENERGY CENTER

ECEPDI ENERGY CENTER

"The building is intended to be a significant example of contemporary architecture. Our building will hold an essential position in this context. Just as buildings in Florence are celebrated for their enduring appeal, I hope our building will also remain relevant and will continue to be admired for the next 100 or 200 years, preserving its youthful significance." — Gu Jin

中国能建
ENERGY CHINA

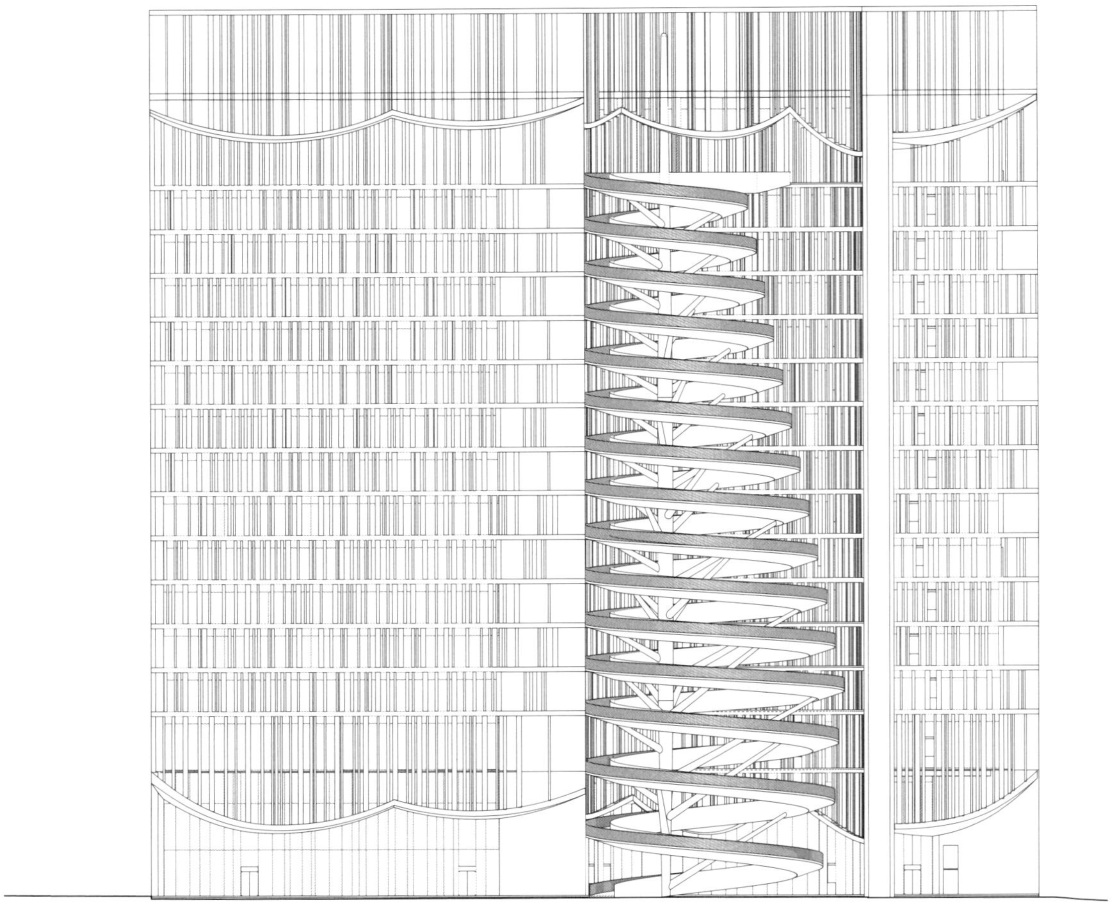

West elevation

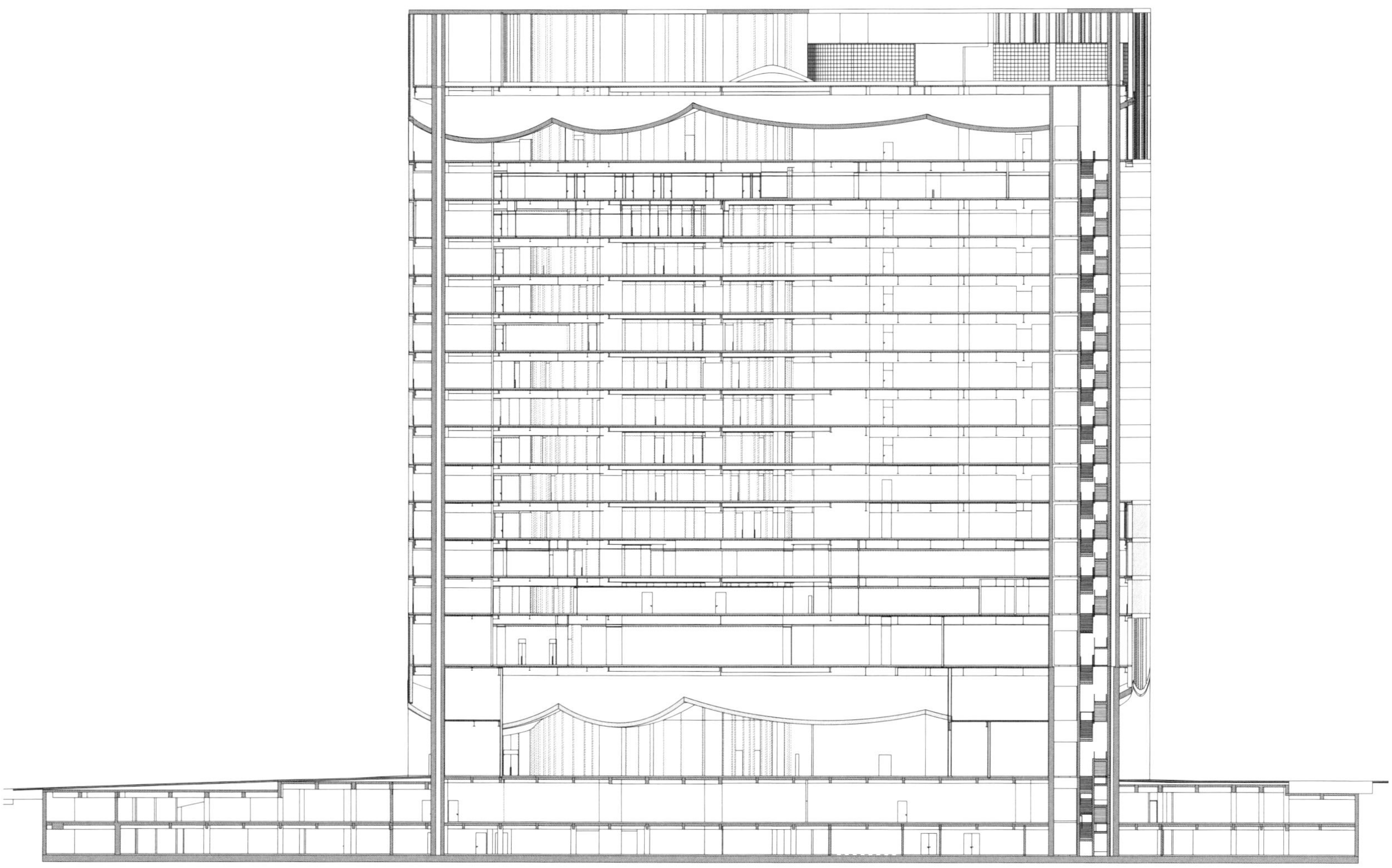

Longitudinal section

0 2 5 10 m

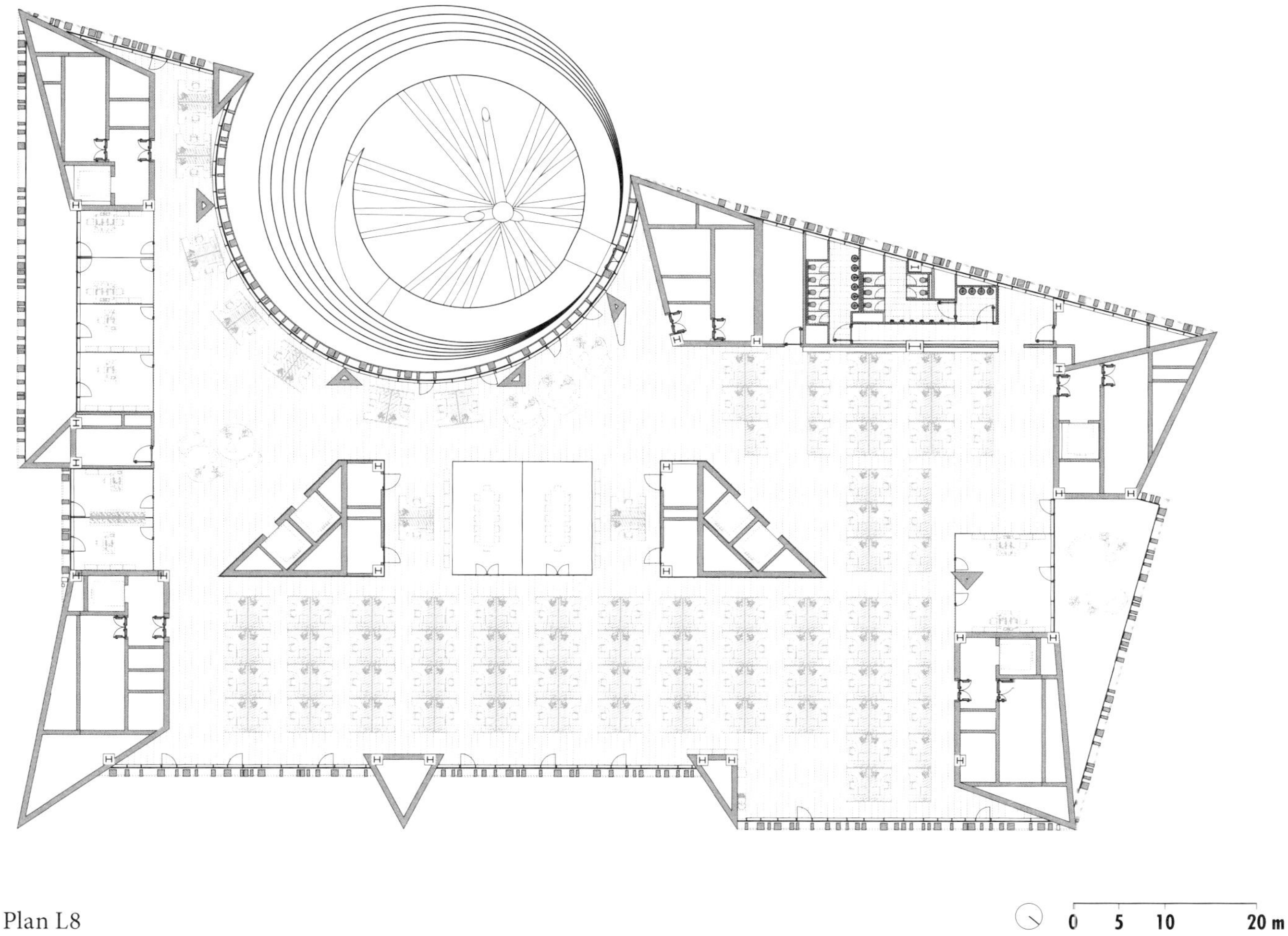

Plan L8

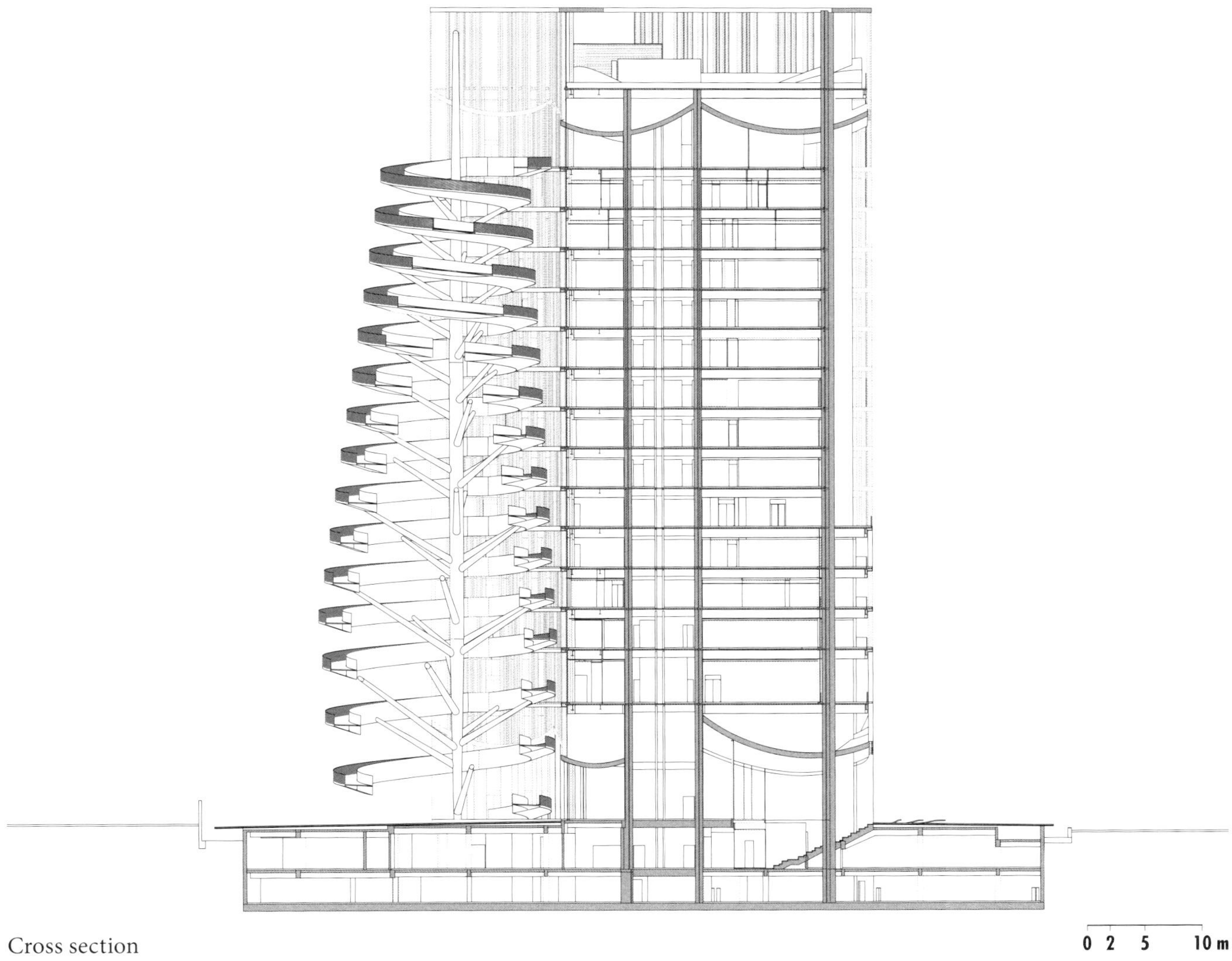

Cross section

2020 Competition winners announced.

02.2021 Demolition of the old ECEPDI office building.

03.2021 A ground-breaking ceremony was held.

2021 The project of the Corten steel ramp was undertaken.

2022 Completed the entire shell and core parts. Cast concrete is the main material of the façade, so completion of this portion was one of the most difficult parts. Materials were ordered for construction of the ramp.

2023 The project has a special, cloudlike ceiling, very difficult to produce, due to its unusual characteristics and curved shape, but it was successfully completed. The large circular Corten steel ramp 1 kilometer in length was installed. Start installation of the façade consisting of a curtain wall and brise soleil.

2024 Work completed in April for opening of the new ECEPDI Shanghai office building.

14,229 sqm plot area

91.5 m height

74,460 sqm total construction area

49,516 sqm above-ground construction area

24,944 underground construction area

15 floors above ground
1 rooftop
2 floors below ground

20.1% percentage of green spaces

HOPE SQUARE BUILDING

OFFICES AND RETAIL

DIANA LIN
STIVEN PENG

DIANA LIN, STIVEN PENG

June 24th 2024 | It all starts from a tree, a very imposing old tree that required the new building to wrap around it and protect it from a metropolis that is rapidly changing. The conversation with Stiven Peng [**SP**] — Former President of TGL (TransGlobe Life Insurance Inc) — and Diana Lin [**DL**] — President of TGL — takes place in the building's penthouse, in a fluid, shady spot that blends with the gardens surrounding it, mitigating the great heat of the day. The clients express their surprise at how this work took form between Taipei and the Renaissance dream of Florence, seeking a fragile balance in the blending of cultures.

LM Welcome. I'm happy to be here with you at Hope Square. Let's start with the name. I was very impressed by the choice of both "hope" and "square." "Hope" means a lot of things related to "time" which is, of course, the time of the future (always unpredictable) and "square," which is a meeting place for people, especially in a city where there are not many squares. Can you tell me more about the naming of this building?

DL Twenty years ago, Taipei experienced a terrible earthquake and, in the aftermath, the government wanted to help the farmers and other people who had suffered. So, having this space, the government named it "Hope" and gave it to those farmers and people so that they would have a place where they could meet, open small businesses, and organize a marketplace. They called it "Hope" then, and we continued that tradition.

This place is devoted to young people to have a look into their future. Also, because it is near Central Art Park, it's a place where people can meet and share new ideas and start their little businesses. So, in this sense, we address "Hope," especially for young people.

LM Fantastic, and what about the term "Square" which is connected to the idea of the vision for the future? I mean, it's more than just a square…

SP When Marco visited this site for the first time, we explored the surroundings: we went to the University, to the Peace Bridge where you can see young people playing basketball or skateboard. Marco told me, "Look at them. Our project must give back to the entire society".

We understood that we needed to design something meaningful. The meaning can probably be summarized by the term "Hope" which is addressed to all the young people here in Taipei. Somehow, this spirit came into this building.

LM That's fantastic. I think if the architecture is good, it creates a good feeling because people easily grow accustomed to beauty and feel compelled to take care of it.

Designing good architecture is a way to improve the general quality of the city and build a stronger sense of community that can arise around this beautiful and meaningful architecture or public spaces.

DL Yes, exactly, this was the starting point. Through our project, we wanted to give back to our community. So, the square is the place where people can relax and enjoy life. We wanted people to come here, look at the beautiful tree, and enjoy the shade it provides to them, but it is also the place where people can rest and enjoy the sense of space.

LM Then we come to the tree, the "number one". We know that the law protects all the trees in the area, which means a higher responsibility for you to continue preserving this crucial natural legacy for this part of the city.

Archea started to design the building around a tree that had to be free to grow inside it. How do you feel about this natural presence? What is your relationship with this particular tree? Why is this tree so important to you?

DL Our business is insurance, and insurance is about people. Every policy we sell is a responsibility that will continue. So, a tree can be seen as a symbol of that sense of responsibility toward living things, let's say, a symbol representing the people. The sense of responsibility and sustainability we provide to ensure that the tree continues to live and grow, became very important. This fact can be very similar to what we do daily with our business: caring for the environment, people, and life.

LM It is a tree that will provide shade for the next generation… a promise for the future.

How did you meet Archea? How did your relationship and collaboration start?

DL We visited Florence, and one of our Italian friends took us to visit Archea's Antinori Winery. We were excited about this beautiful structure and were introduced to Marco Casamonti. Immediately, we were very impressed with Marco's ideas and approach to designing a building like that, a winery designed for the next century.

At that time, we had to start this project in Taipei, and we thought Marco and Archea would be the right choice because we also needed a building designed for the next century.

LM What were the requests you made to Marco? What was the key request for designing this building?

SP When you come to Taiwan, the first building you see is the 101, because it is the tallest building. That being the case, I told Marco we didn't want a taller building but a meaningful one that people would remember for a long time. Years before, Marco had asked the owner of Antinori what sort of winery he had in mind, and had received more or less the same answer: a winery that would last into the next century.

I know Marco can deliver more than a design proposal, but also the means to carry it forward. And that is how our collaboration began.

It strikes me that, while we have been developing commercial buildings for the past twenty years, this is the first building I have ever acquired by getting a recommendation from a friend about someone I didn't know. So I have to thank Archea for contributing this building to Taipei City because it is now one of the most important buildings here.

We evidently had the right idea and Marco has designed something that significantly benefits us all.

LM I can imagine. This is not like creating new boxes. This is a landmark now but it will last in time, contributing to change the character of the entire city. This proves that things can be done differently without making offices like boxes…

SP It's interesting that you mention "boxes". When we first designed this building, from a financial and corporate perspective, the return of global operation was essential to us. We considered the best way to create offices in a "box". When we designed this building with a great curve to preserve the tree, we assumed that the usage rate would be the lowest. But before this building was finished, we realized how the company's mentality had changed, because people wanted to work in this kind of building, sharing this atmosphere. I think something changed with this building…

DL When we discussed this building with Marco, he told us that, when we talk about a building, we are talking about an object that relates to the land it is built on, the society in which it is located, the people who will occupy it, the past, and the future. These connections opened our minds, and we knew that we were looking for a building that could connect our past, especially to this site that where the government once dedicated to the suffering population and the future. I believe Marco was the right person to transform something very conceptual, like this idea, into something authentic and livable.

LM This is a real challenge because society is changing so rapidly, and working habits are changing too. People want to work in places that seem "homier" and have a stronger "domestic" connotation. In this sense, the quality of the space is very important, and I'm sure that the people working here are much more excited to do what they do than if they were closed into conventional "boxes". Don't you think so?

DL Yes, indeed. We have got so much positive feedback from our tenants…

LM Let's talk about this beautiful curved building. I can imagine how this was a delightful idea but, at the same time, a serious problem. Environmentally speaking, the building is certainly clever and the curve creates shade. This probably was part of a discussion about sustainability…

SP We talked about how we could relate the building to the environment: the lines of trees and the lines of the glass façade… Everything is connected to the sky. You can see how the building plays into its environment. I think that is what Marco had in mind during our first meeting.

DL As you mentioned before, this beautiful curve was also a problem, however. The curve was incredibly challenging to build. Marco Casamonti and the local architects, who had to realize it, had a lot of discussion about how to do it, how to transform those beautiful drawings into something tangible. Above all, we had to think about expenses because building this curve increased the costs. We needed to find a balance, reconsidering the overall cost of the construction…

LM Obviously, you found the right solutions, and the result is fantastic… The steel structure becomes thinner and more transparent as it rises, and the density of the façade decreases and appears to evaporate into the air and the sky…

DL This façade is very beautiful. It's not only about the curve but also about the building's general transparency, which allows us to see what is going on at different times of the day: the lighting and the reflections are always different.

LM We always say that good architecture is meteorological architecture, in that it changes its image with the variation of light and darkness. The building reflects and reacts to the changing seasons directly on its body.

SP Another interesting fact is that every architect has his own idea. This creates conflicts, although I would prefer to call them alternative ways of thinking.

This happened between Marco's ideas and our local architects, who had to realize the building according to our local rules and prescriptions…

LM How did the Italians and Taiwanese blend?

DL There were inevitably numerous conflicts between the local regulations and Marco's ideas. I think that is fairly normal. My job is to adapt the designer's ideas, even more so when they are foreign, to our local laws and building regulations, always trying to do my best to deliver a building that respects the designer's original idea as much as possible.

LM How do the Italian and Taiwanese cultures blend in this building? What do you think are the more Taiwanese or Italian looking parts of this building?

SP We are both family-oriented. Whenever we go to Italy, we recognize the way people discuss issues…

LM We have similar local food…

DL Yes, it's true. Food is so important in your culture, and it's the same here. We are also very enthusiastic, as you are. So, I feel a real connection between our countries.

LM There is an interesting relationship between the interior and the exterior of the building. You can talk about being "in and out": the city's landscape, the mountains around it, and the interior spaces in the building somehow participate in each other. Something is happening in this place: here we are on the rooftop, and it is a lovely garden.

Can you tell me more about this unique space? It's like a city inside a building, with squares, gardens…

SP We usually have gala dinners up here. Unlike other squared balconies, the shape is more open here, going around like a garden. It's so pleasant to stroll outside while having dinner and enjoying our guests…

DL What I love about this place is that you don't realize the length of the balcony when you look outside. It's a surprise when the space suddenly opens out before you; it's really stunning. It always surprises our guests: the path starts narrow and then opens up again…

LM That is the power of using curves: you can never see the end, and the walkway becomes a real spatial experience. Every time you go out there, you discover something surprising, a wonder. I think this is a real place of wonder: you have a building that is a garden, a square, both private and public…

I'd like to know more about the future of this landmark and the future of your company. How do you see the vision expressed by this building and what does it say about the future of your company?

DL We are working on a second project with Marco. It's outside the Taipei Airport. It's another curved building that reminds me of a beautiful butterfly that has just emerged from its cocoon and is ready to fly away. That's the initial concept, representing our company, which is ready to grow after an important merger and ten years of transition. Our company is ready for the next stage.

LM I think it's a wonderful idea to mark every new stage with meaningful, iconic architecture. I look forward to seeing the next building!

SITE	Taipei, Taiwan [N 25°2'42.471" E 121°31'56.411"]
PROGRAM	Offices and retail
DIMENSIONS	Area: 7,600 sqm Covered area: 3,000 sqm
CHRONOLOGY	2016-2021
CLIENT	TransGlobe Life Insurance Inc.
ARCHITECTURAL PROJECT AND ART DIRECTION	Archea / Marco Casamonti: Laura Andreini Marco Casamonti Silvia Fabi Giovanni Polazzi
PROJECT COORDINATOR	Francesco Giordani
ARCHITECTURAL PROJECT TEAM	Giovanni Amadu, Francesca Cardinale, Federica Ferraro, Marco Gamberi, Gao Ying
LOCAL ARCHITECT	TMA architects & associates; LIN+ ARCHITECTS
STRUCTURAL DESIGN	ENVISION Engineering Consultants
DESIGN OF INSTALLATIONS	Idee Engineering Consulting Co. Ltd.
GENERAL CONSTRUCTION COMPANY	RUENTEX Engineering & Construction Co. Ltd

全球人壽

The homogeneous urban fabric contributes to the crowdedness of Taipei city, where it is difficult to find large buildings: narrow streets and small lots shape the urban fabric.
The design for Hope Square Building exhibits a strong iconic and recognizable geometric form, inspired by the necessity to protect and enhance the presence of a non-disruptable line of trees. A fully glazed volume in essence appears to have a homogeneous and continuous surface, is enhanced further with the retreat of the structure and the stringcourse. The pre-existing tree line has been safeguarded and enhanced by excavating the center of building for the entirety of its height. This solution is amplified and made evident even along all the elevations visible from the main roads of the area, through terraces that excavate the volume and bring light to mid-sized trees planted in hanging gardens. This concept finds its conclusion in the large roof garden, which can be visited on the top floor. The subtraction of volumes, to create different exedras at different heights was also used to shape the 3 plant floors on the roof, which draw a different skyline from any point you look at this building. Taipei's buildings have a unique characteristic: the existence of different spheres between the ground and upper floors. In fact, the project encompasses different functions where the lower floors and the basement are home to retail activities, while above, are arranged offices for 5 floors and a penthouse. Aiming to give slenderness to the building as whole while also providing protection to the visitors of the garden, the crowning of the façade at the roof is decorated by a brise-soleil, which also functions as a protective screen for the view of the plants. Made from a sparse stave of square section tubes, it is arranged along all the facades of the building by means of a white silk-screen printing, in bands of different widths, creating a play of light refraction throughout the building. The use of soft and sinuous lines, contrasted with the hardness and regularity of the facade create a unique contrast: a large building while simultaneously light and bright, a shimmering and elusive geometry that creates a fascinating optical illusion.

2016 | 2021

HOPE SQUARE BUILDING

"This façade is very beautiful. It's not only about the curve but also about the building's general transparency, which allows us to see what is going on at different times of the day: the lighting and the reflections are always different." — Diana Lin

"The square is the place where people can relax and enjoy life. We wanted people to come here, look at the beautiful tree, and enjoy the shade it provides to them, but it is also the place where people can rest and enjoy the sense of space." — Diana Lin

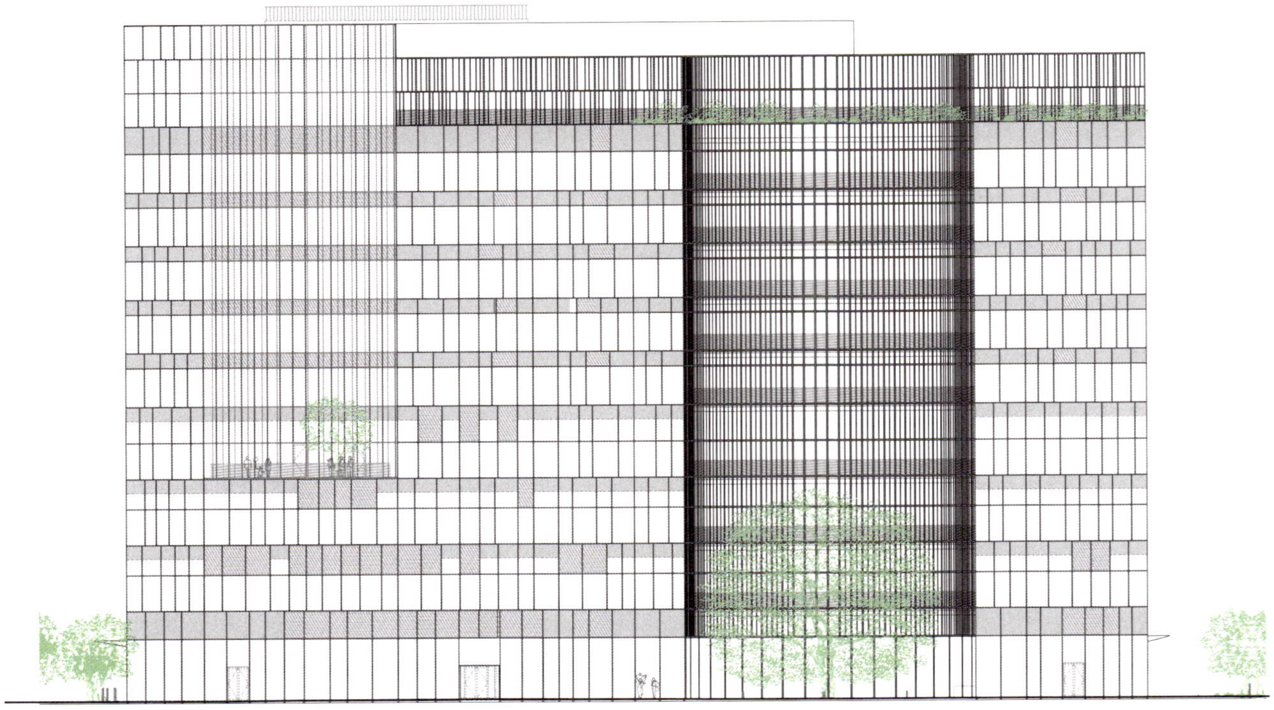

North elevation

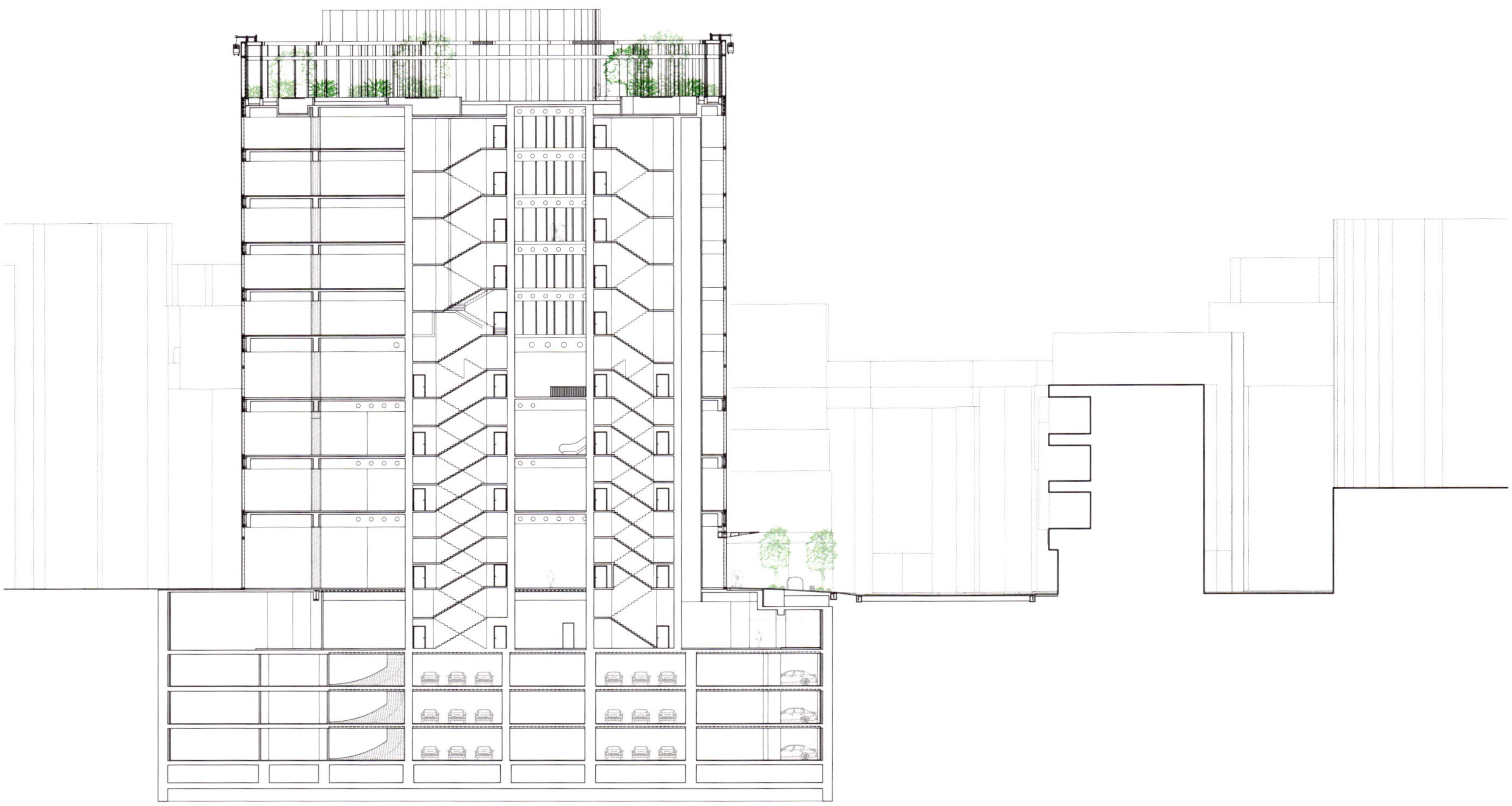

Cross section

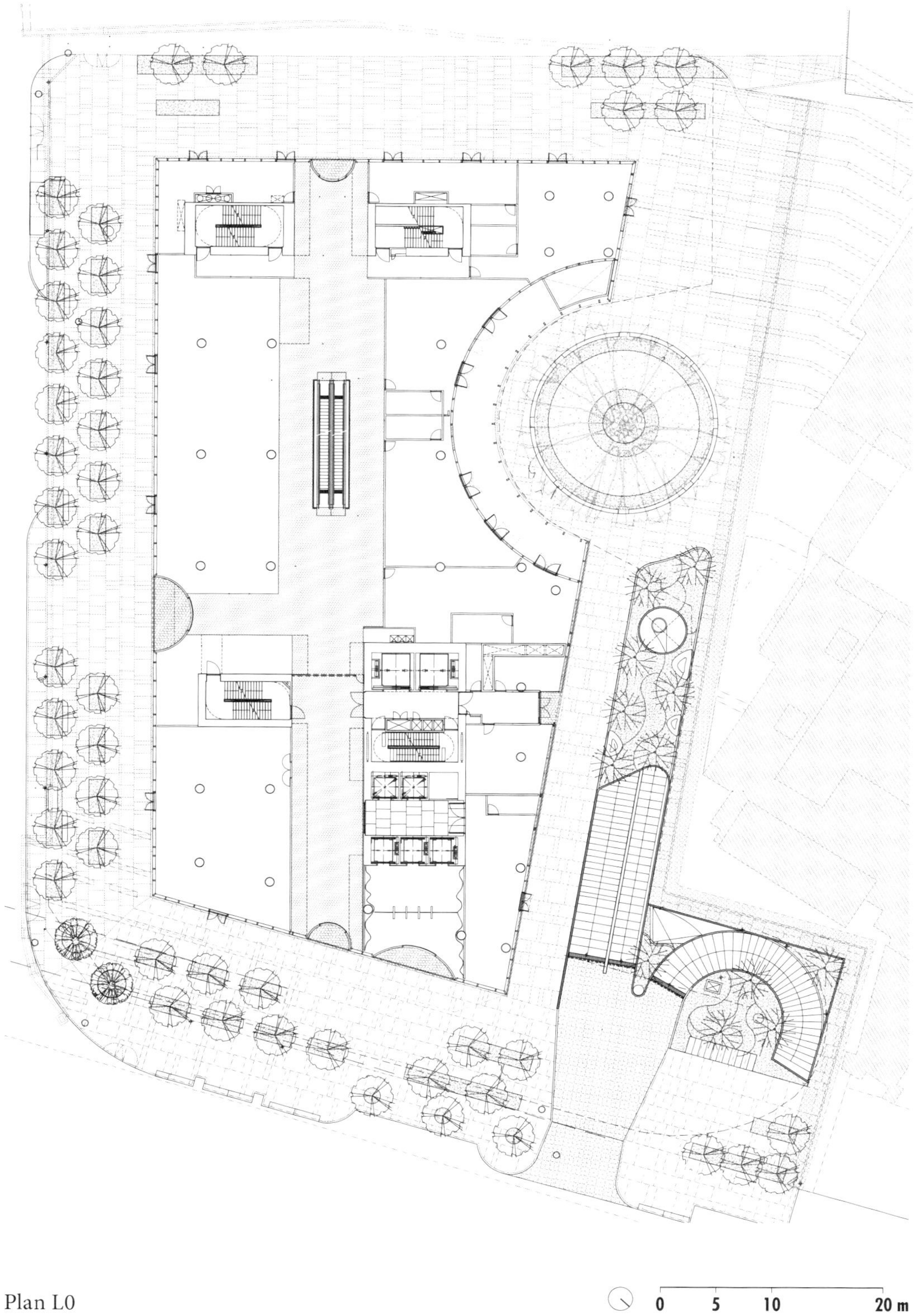

Plan L0

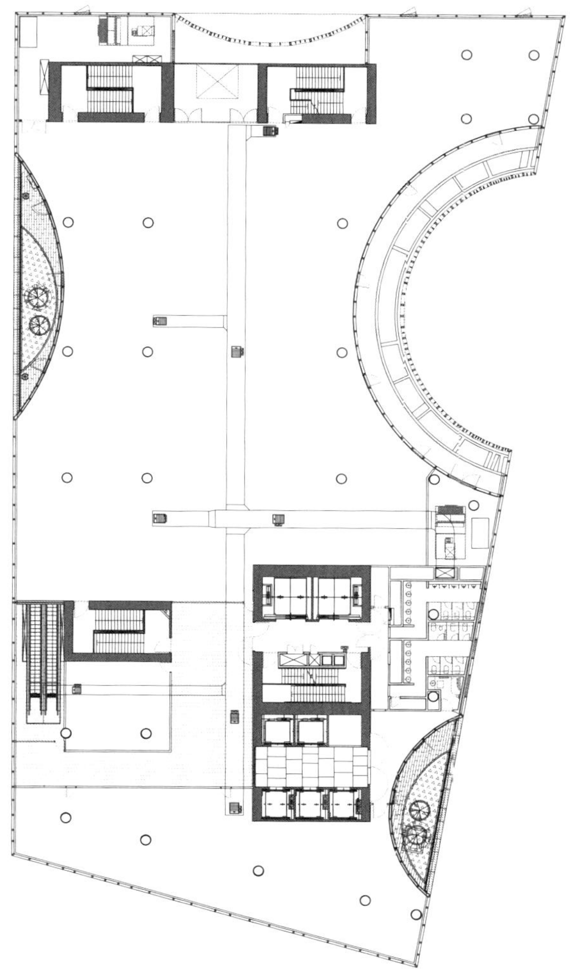

Plan L4

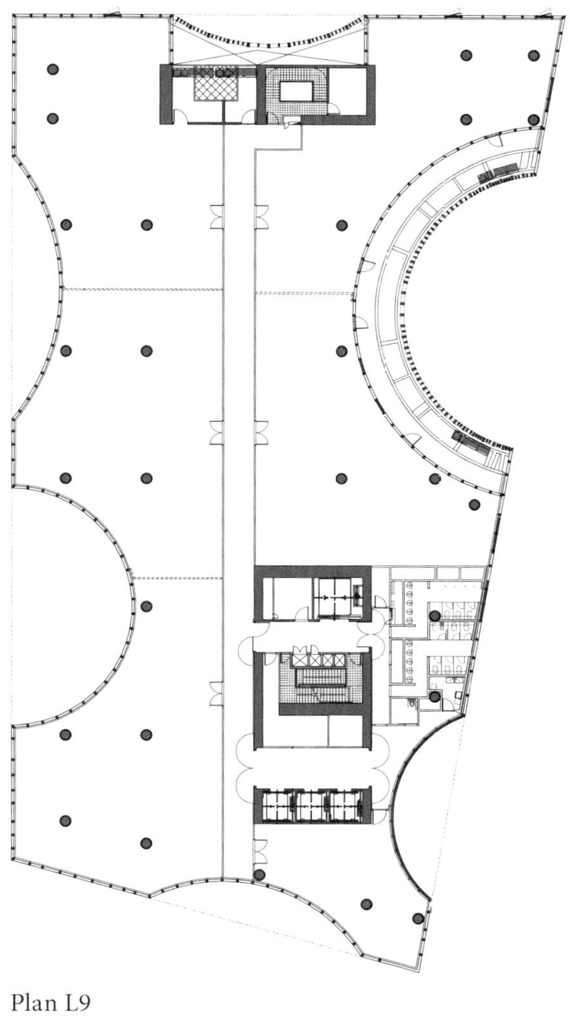

Plan L9

 HOPE SQUARE BUILDING

Panasonic
光華數位新天地

03.2016 Already during the stages of inspection of the site and negotiation of contract terms, a series of freehand drawings were made, graphically representing some of the composition concepts arising from meetings with the client, who stressed the need to create an iconic building that would also open up new urban spatiality, contributing to the socio-economic development of the area.

12.2016 Presentation of the preliminary project, characterized by a structure where the ground floor and belvedere terrace are considered fully public spaces, open to all.

06.2017 After reaching an understanding and exchanging opinions over an extended period, the client, the designers, consultants and representatives of the urban planning department of the city of Taipei, reached agreement and the draft project was revised with a variant to improve the functionality of the spaces which, following approval, was developed as a final project.

09.2018 After the final project had obtained the approval of the local administrators, the worksite area was prepared. The start of the activity was celebrated with a "ground-breaking" ceremony attended by the clients, the architects, the construction company and the authorities. During the event, to ensure the successful outcome of the work, each of the key players in the construction process dug a symbolic shovelful of soil which was piled into a heap for good luck.

10.2019 While construction of the underground portions was going on, the final project of the parts above ground was completed, with particular attention to the design of the façade. To ensure its ability to resist typhoons and earthquakes, a 1:1 scale replica was built of a portion of the corner of the façade, 15 meters wide and 3 meters high, which was stressed in a sort of wind tunnel. The outcome of the trial was positive at the first test.

12.2019 The same portion of the façade was then tested to verify the exterior aspect and architectural propriety of the building. The textural and chromatic choices made for the sample were the same ones effectively used.

06.2020 After completing the structure, a fundamental event in the construction of the building was celebrated with the "beam-raising" ceremony on occasion of laying the last structural element necessary to complete the structure.

11.2021 Completion of construction of the building.

143,900 cu. m	above ground
53 m	height
7,600 sqm	lot area
3,000 sqm	covered area
21,272 sqm	underground area
28,048 sqm	above ground area
4,600 sqm	exterior area
54,000 sqm	total built area
12,450 sqm	area of the continuous glass façade
2,850	no. of cells of the façade

HOPE SQUARE BUILDING

KEEP

PRIVATE HOME IN VIA FRUSA	Florence, Italy	1988
NEW OFFICES STUDIO ARCHEA, LUNGARNO B. CELLINI	Florence, Italy	1991
DESIGN FOR A RESIDENTIAL AND ARTISAN CENTER	Castiglioncello, Livorno, Italy	1992
DESIGN FOR A MASTERPLAN FOR THE SDO, EASTERN BUSINESS AND ADMINISTRATIVE SYSTEM OF ROME	Rome, Italy	1992
STOP LINE. CENTER FOR ENTERTAINMENT AND DINING	Curno, Bergamo, Italy	1994-1995
PLAN FOR AREA OF MONS. NATALE BASILICO, SQUARE AND PARKING AREA	Merate, Lecco, Italy	1996
SINGLE-FAMILY PRIVATE HOME IN LEFFE	Bergamo, Italy	1997
SWIMMING POOL IN VAL SERIANA	Bergamo, Italy	1997
VILLA IN GAZZANIGA	Bergamo, Italy	1998
PIER CAPPONI OFFICE CENTER	Florence, Italy	1998
QLÒ DISCO IN FIESOLE	Florence, Italy	1998
URBAN IMPROVEMENT PLAN FOR TAVERNUZZE	Tavarnuzze, Florence, Italy	1999
EXPANSION OF PORT OF FONTVILLE	Fontville, Montecarlo	1999
REMODELING OF TORNABUONI ARTE	Portofino, Genova, Italy	2000
DESIGN FOR A MULTI-USE CULTURAL CENTER	Merate, Lecco, Italy	2000
BODY'S GYM	Florence, Italy	2001
REMODELING AND CONVERSION OF FORMER OFFICINE LENZI	Lucca, Italy	2001
BOTTAI PARKING, BICYCLE AND PEDESTRIAN PATH, ENVIRONMENTAL LANDSCAPING AND RESTORATION OF PALI PARK AREA, PEDESTRIAN OVERPASS	Florence, Italy	2001
EXECUTIVE DESIGN MILAN-NAPLES HIGHWAY. RESTORATION, LANDSCAPING AND ENVIRONMENTAL INCLUSION	Impruneta, Florence, Italy	2001
DESIGN FOR INSTALLING SOUND-ABSORBING BARRIERS ON A SECTION OF THE MILAN-NAPLES HIGHWAY	Italy	2001
PROJECT FOR THE REDEVELOPMENT IN VIA TIRRENO	Potenza, Italy	2001
RESIDENTIAL AND COMMERCIAL CENTER	Tavarnuzze, Florence, Italy	2001
DESIGN OF THE MARTINI ILLUMINAZIONE SPA STAND AT EUROLUCE	Milan, Italy	2001
EXECUTIVE DESIGN OF THE MILAN-NAPLES HIGHWAY FOR PROJECTS IN THE IMPRUNETA AND SCANDICCI AREAS. TRANSPORTATION HUB OF CERTOSA AREA	Florence, Italy	2001
NEW GRANITIFIANDRE SHOWROOM	Castellarano, Reggio Emilia, Italy	2001-2002
THE CORD. ENTRANCE 50TH VENICE BIENNALE	Venice, Italy	2003
DESIGN OF THE CULTURAL EVENT "ENZIMI"	Rome, Italy	2003
URBAN RENEWAL OF SALAROLI AREA	Cesena, Italy	2003

SCHEMATIC DESIGN FOR AN OLYMPIC VILLAGE IN DOHA FOR THE ASIAN GAMES 2006	Doha, Qatar	2004
RENEWAL PROJECT FOR VIA CESARE BATTISTI	Cesena, Italy	2004
DESIGN FOR A NEW DIVISION IN LOC. DIACCETO	Pelago, Florence, Italy	2005
UNDERGROUND PARKING BEHIND PALAZZO TETTAMANTI	Merate, Lecco, Italy	2005
BORGO ARNOLFO. NEW RESIDENTIAL AND COMMERCIAL CENTER OF THE FORMER ALBERTI HOSPITAL	San Giovanni Valdarno, Florence, Italy	2006
DESIGN FOR EXHIBITION-EVENT "VINAR VINO, ARTE E ARCHITETTURA", STAZIONE LEOPOLDA	Florence, Italy	2006
DESIGN FOR NEW OFFICES OF THE ITALIAN CHAMBER OF COMMERCE IN BEIJING	Beijing, China	2006
RENOVATION AND EXPANSION OF A VILLA	Bagno a Ripoli, Florence, Italy	2006
ALBATROS CAMPING	San Vincenzo, Livorno, Italy	2006
PUBLIC LIBRARY	Nembro, Italy	2002-2007
DISCO TANGO	Beijing, China	2006-2007
NEW OFFICES FOR MARCO POLO COMPANY	Beijing, China	2006-2007
ANNALI DELL'ARCHITETTURA E DELLE CITTÀ, PALAZZO REALE	Naples, Italy	2007
BICU. PUB AND RESTAURANT	Genoa, Italy	2007
CONVENTIONAL RESIDENTIAL HOUSING PROJECT	Sesto Fiorentino, Florence, Italy	2007
PRELIMINARY DESIGN FOR THE MANIFATTURE TABACCHI AREA FOR PIRELLI SPA	Milan, Italy	2007
PUG - GENERAL URBAN PLAN FOR BISCEGLIE	Bisceglie, Bari, Italy	2007
ZHUZHOU COMMERCIAL BUILDINGS	Zhuzhou, China	2007
STOOLCASE FURNITURE DESIGN	Beijing, China	2007
PARKOUR – BEIJING. RESIDENTIAL AND COMMERCIAL CENTER	Beijing, China	2007
MILANOFIORI 2000. PROJECT FOR A RESIDENTIAL SUBDIVISION	Assago, Milan, Italy	2007
DESIGN FOR THE "TORRE DELLE ARTI"	Milan, Italy	2007
PRELIMINARY DESIGN FOR THE MANIFATTURE SIGARO TOSCANO AREA	Cava dei Tirreni, Salerno, Italy	2007
THE FORMER LAZZERI THEATER	Livorno, Italy	2003-2008
NEW MASTERPLAN FOR TRIPOLI	Tripoli, Lybia	2008
DESIGN FOR THE FORTE CARLO FELICE RESIDENCE, LA MADDALENA	Olbia-Tempio, Sassari, Italy	2008
STATE POLICE MULTI-USE CENTER	Naples, Italy	2008
DESIGN FOR A TOWER	Modena, Italy	2008
ANNALI DELL'ARCHITETTURA E DELLE CITTÀ, PALAZZO REALE	Naples, Italy	2008
MUNICIPAL LIBRARY AND AUDITORIUM	Curno, Italy	1999-2009

DESIGN FOR THE NEW BIRRA PERONI HEADQUARTERS	Rome, Italy	2007-2009
DESIGN FOR THE KPM TOWER	Dubai, United Arab Emirates	2009
ART CUBE	Casalbeltrame, Novara, Italy	2009
NEW UNIVERSITY OF TRIPOLI	Tripoli, Lybia	2009
DESIGN FOR MERAVIGLIOSA ISLAND "THE WORLD"	Dubai, United Arab Emirates	2009
DESIGN FOR EX MANIFATTURA SIGARO TOSCANO	Foiano della Chiana, Arezzo, Italy	2009
UBPA B3-2 PAVILION EXPO 2010	Shanghai, China	2007-2010
METROPOLITAN. MULTI-USE COMPLEX	Livorno, Italy	2005-2011
FIRENZE NOVA. RESIDENTIAL COMPLEX	Florence, Italy	2006-2011
PERFETTI VAN MELLE FACTORY	Lainate, Italy	2005-2011
CDD DAILY CENTER FOR DISABILITY	Seregno, Italy	2003-2012
GEL GREEN ENERGY LABORATORY	Shanghai, China	2008-2012
DWELLINGS IN VIA MAESTRI CAMPIONESI	Milan, Italy	2009-2012
LE TERRAZZE	Cunardo, Italy	2010-2012
ANTINORI NEL CHIANTI CLASSICO WINERY	San Casciano Val di Pesa, Italy	2004-2013
TORNABUONI ARTE	Florence, Italy	2013
INTERNATIONAL GRAPE EXHIBITION GARDEN	Beijing, China	2011-2014
SAN LORENZO CENTRAL MARKET	Florence, Italy	2013-2014
LILING WORLD CERAMIC ART CITY	Liling, China	2010-2015
SANTO STEFANO. REHABILITATION INSTITUTE	Potenza Picena, Italy	2012-2015
RUA HARMONIA	Sao Paulo, Brazil	2013-2015
PRIVATE HOUSE IN PIETRASANTA	Lucca, Italy	2015
COLLE LORETO	Lugano, Switzerland	2011-2016
DACIA ARENA, CLADDING	Udine, Italy	2014-2016
BENCI HOUSE	Florence, Italy	2016
MOYO. AMERICAN BAR	Florence, Italy	2016
EATALY STORE. FORMER WINE WAREHOUSE	Trieste, Italy	2012-2017
TONGJI UNIVERSITY	Shanghai, China	2015-2017
IS-SUQ TAL-BELT VALLETTA FOOD MARKET	La Valletta, Malta	2015-2018
FORNACE SUITE	Florence, Italy	2016-2018
SANLORENZO HEADQUARTERS	La Spezia, Italy	2016-2018
TSH THE STUDENT HOTEL	Florence, Italy	2016-2018
LUCE DI CARRARA	Seravezza, Italy	2018
VILLA APOLLINA	Ibiza, Spain	2018-2019

EX AREA FIAT	Florence, Italy	2019
EX CERAMICA LAGO AREA	Laveno-Mombello, Italy	2006-2020
THE VEIL	Astana, Kazakhstan	2015-2020
GRAND UNIVERSE HOTEL	Lucca, Italy	2016-2020
HAND PRODUCTION BUILDING. SALVATORE FERRAGAMO FACTORY	Florence, Italy	2019-2020
TORNABUONI ART GALLERY	Paris, France	2019-2020
AIR ALBANIA STADIUM	Tirana, Albania	2016-2021
HOPE SQUARE BUILDING	Taipei, Taiwan	2016-2021
RIFUGIO DIGITALE	Florence, Italy	2022
ALBAN TOWER	Tirana, Albania	2005-2023
ROCCO B. COMMISSO VIOLA PARK	Florence, Italy	2021-2023
GARDEN BUILDING	Tirana, Albania	2018-2024
KISS BRIDGE	Phú Quốc, Vietnam	2019-2024
ECEPDI ENERGY CENTER	Shanghai, China	2021-2024

NIA STA

Laura Andreini, Marco Casamonti, and Giovanni Polazzi, graduates of the School of Architecture of the University of Florence, Italy, founded Studio Archea in the same city in 1988. Their practice grew and developed, and in 2001 Silvia Fabi joined them in creating Archea Associati. Over the years they have brought numerous international works to completion and opened ateliers in Europe, China, the United Arab Emirates, Brazil, and Albania.

Alongside their main activities in experimental architecture and in the realization of works on a wide range of scales – from objects to buildings and urban planning – they have also been occupied with research and teaching activities in the field of architectural design at various Italian universities. In particular, Marco Casamonti is Full Professor of Architectural and Urban Design at the Faculty of Architecture of the University of Genoa, while Laura Andreini holds the Chair of Architectural and Urban Design at the School of Architecture of the University of Florence. Their professional practice has always been accompanied by in-depth studies and critical reflection, disseminated by means of essays and other writings in books and magazines in Italy and abroad, and the organization of exhibitions, events, and workshops in the realm of architectural design. Since 1997, Marco Casamonti has been the editor of the international architectural magazine Area, with Laura Andreini as deputy editor since 2002. It is currently published by the group Tecniche Nuove, in Milan. From 2006 to 2008, Casamonti was scientific editor of Fondazione Annali dell'Architettura e delle Città, in Naples. Since 2009, Laura Andreini has been the editor of Forma Edizioni, a publisher specialized in art, architecture, design, and photography.

The firm has created a series of works that have been published in books and the principal international magazines, and selected for important architectural exhibitions.

Archea Associati has participated in many of the most important national and international architecture competitions and consultations, winning numerous prizes and awards. Their designs for the high-speed railway stations in Turin and Florence were selected in 2001 and 2002. In 2003, they were among the nine Italian design studios commissioned by Immobiliare Novoli for the realisation of a large urban block in the former Fiat area in Florence. In 2004, in collaboration with architect Rafael Moneo, the studio participated in the competition by invitation for the design of the new Palazzo del Cinema in Venice. In 2005 it won thecompetition by invitation for the design of the Alban Tower, a tower included in the masterplanfor the redevelopment of the centre of Tirana.

In 2007, he took part in the competition for the executive design and execution of the worksfor the Park of Music and Culture in Florence and was awarded second place.

In 2014, the Antinori nel Chianti Classico winery was the protagonist of the exhibition Innesti atthe 14th International Architecture Exhibition of the Venice Biennale. In 2018 their project for a house/studio in Rua Harmonia in São Paulo, Brazil, was exhibited at the MetropoliNovissima exhibition, organised by the Fondazione Annali dell'Architettura e delle Città di Napoli.

In 2023 they won the Competition for the Redevelopment of the Antico Borgo di Castelnuovo in Avane and were selected by NEOM to design part of The Line project.

Among the most important completed projects, in addition to those already mentioned, are the UBPA B3-2 Pavilion in the Urban Best Practices area of Expo 2010 Shanghai; the World Ceramic Art City in Liling, China; Hope Square Building in Taipei; the Colle Loreto residential building in Lugano, Switzerland; the renovation of the Former Wine Warehouse in Trieste and its transformation into Eataly; The Air Albania Stadium in Albania; the renovation and transformation of the Mercato Centrale in Florence and the Is-Suq Tal-Belt Valletta Food Market in Malta; the TSH Florence Lavagnini and the transformation of the Hand production Building. Salvatore Ferragamo factory, both in Florence; the Universe Hotel in Lucca for the Marriott Group – Autograph Collection; and the construction of The Veil in Astana (Nur-Sultan), Kazakhstan, which houses restaurants, stores and a boutique hotel, complete with spa. The Antinori nel Chianti Classico winery in Bargino, opened in 2012 and climbed the world podium by receiving the World's Best Vineyards 2022 award, ranking first among the world's best wine tourism excellences. In 2023, the Alban Tower in Tirana and the large sports centre Viola Park Rocco B. Commisso in Bagno a Ripoli (Florence) while in 2024, ECEPDI Energy Center: the new headquarters of ECEPDI in Shanghai is inaugurated.

Currently under construction are the redevelopment of the Sea Square in Durres, Albania, and the above-mentioned Ponte di Legno Spa Center in Brescia, among others.

The firm also has major projects in the design phase, including the Bà Nà Winery in Vietnam. The new Kiss Bridge is already completed. The design for the LeoFrance plant in Florence is in the final stages, and a master plan for the Kastrati Group, in Tirana, with hotels, office towers, and a shopping center.

First printed in October 2024
by ABC Tipografia, Calenzano, Italy